DARWIN'S LEGACY

NOBEL CONFERENCE XVIII

Gustavus Adolphus College, St. Peter, Minnesota

Darwin's Legacy

◆

Edited by Charles L. Hamrum

With Contributions by Stephen Jay Gould,
Irving Stone, Richard E. Leakey,
Sir Peter B. Medawar, Edward O. Wilson,
and Jaroslav Pelikan

1817

Harper & Row, Publishers, San Francisco

Cambridge, Hagerstown, New York, Philadelphia
London, Mexico City, São Paulo, Sydney

FIRST EDITION

Designer: Jim Mennick

Library of Congress Cataloging in Publication Data

Nobel Conference (18th : 1982 : Gustavus Adolphus College)
⎺DARWIN'S LEGACY.

  Held Oct. 5–6, 1982.
  Contents: In praise of Charles Darwin / Stephen Jay
Gould — The human mind after Darwin / Irving Stone —
African origins / Richard E. Leakey— [etc.]
  1. Human evolution—Congresses. 2. Darwin, Charles, 1809–1882—Congresses. I. Hamrum, Charles L. II. Gould, Stephen Jay. III. Title.
GN281.N6 1982   573.2   83–47723
ISBN 0–06–250651–X

---

83 84 85 86 87 10 9 8 7 6 5 4 3 2 1

To Edgar M. Carlson

Contents

Preface

Each year an aura of anticipation is reflected by the people on the Gustavus Adolphus College campus as the annual Nobel Conference nears. However, as Nobel Conference XVIII approached, everyone behaved as though he or she were about to hear from Dean Witter. Everyone had at least one hero among the conference participants, and this elevated the general expectations of the entire campus community.

Nor were the lofty expectations for this conference confined to the immediate vicinity of St. Peter. Students and faculty from high schools and colleges from Minnesota and nearby states, as well as a delegation from the People's Republic of China, joined the many veteran visitors of previous Nobel Conferences in Lund Arena for this interpretation of *Darwin's Legacy*. It was indeed a tribute to the conference participants, who, with Darwin, responded by effectively reminding us that our minds have changed and will continue to do so.

A conference such as this does not happen without the selfless gifts of toil, inspiration, and dedication of a great many people. The 1982 Nobel committee gratefully thanks these nameless, but all-important faculty, staff persons, and students who really produce the conference. Special recognition is accorded to those who made the conference possible—such as the Russell Lunds, the Nobel Foundation, John Kendall, Robert Peterson, Elaine Brostrom, and Conference Director

Richard Elvee of Gustavus Adolphus College—to Clayton Carlson of Harper & Row, and particularly to Edgar M. Carlson, who conceived of a Nobel Conference series and established this worthy tradition.

CHARLES L. HAMRUM, Chairman
Nobel Conference XVIII

Introduction

The contents of this volume were originally presented at Nobel Conference XVIII, October 5 and 6, 1982, on the campus of Gustavus Adolphus College in St. Peter, Minnesota. The Nobel Conferences originated following an event in 1963, when the college dedicated its new science building as an American memorial to Alfred Nobel, with twenty-six laureates in attendance. Two years later, the Nobel Foundation authorized the organization of an ongoing conference in Nobel's name, to deal with scientific and social concerns. Large audiences have attended these conferences, which have always featured leading scientists of the world and renowned thinkers in other disciplines. We at Gustavus are pleased to present the proceedings of Nobel Conference XVIII, *Darwin's Legacy*.

Charles Darwin died on April 19, 1882, leaving a world shaken by his revolutionary revelations of natural biotic processes through time. His effect on the Western mind has periodically been assessed. Therefore, on this occasion, one hundred years after his death, it seemed fitting and natural to re-examine his influence on how we view our place in nature. We believe that our response to the centenary of this great thinker's death was both appropriate and appreciated.

Our preliminary preparation for Nobel Conference XVIII quickly reinforced our original belief that Darwin's "legacy" was still of interest. The "scientific" creationist movement, in concert with the general "New Right" coalition, had revived the polarization Darwin precipitated with his publication of *The Origin of Species* in 1859. In short order, we were able to assemble a remarkable group of scholars to discuss Darwin's legacy.

In an extemporaneous lecture, Stephen Jay Gould brilliantly described why it was so difficult for the Western mind to become reconciled with natural selection theory. He acknowledged that we are usually able to deal with the fact of evolution, particularly if applied to plants or to other animals, but that we are furnished with strong cultural biases against the notion that nature has also selected us. We are comfortable, Gould stated, with a world in which all organisms fit into their environments and all environments somehow fit into the world. An evolutionary mechanism *without* a gradual, progressive sequence determined by causal events does not appeal to us. Such a system of change assumes that we, along with the rest of life, merely represent a set of historically contingent accidents. He praised Darwin as a true revolutionary thinker with remarkable insight into living systems. Darwin was, and still is, the linchpin of evolutionary thought.

Irving Stone shared his rich knowledge of Darwin's life and times as he presented his paper, "The Human Mind After Darwin," to an audience of about four thousand people. In this address, which opened the conference, Dr. Stone equated many of the rapid advances in various fields of endeavor with the liberating new view of life presented by Darwin.

A fascinating review of hominid history was interpreted from the fossil record by Richard Leakey. Paleoanthropologist Leakey urged his audience to regard themselves as members of a species and to be concerned with managing our planet so that the *species* may survive, rather than just a particular part of the species. In his proposed classification of the Hominidae, he suggested that the genus *Homo* be applied to any bipedal ape and that skull characteristics be used to separate the species. His wit and wisdom completely captivated his audience.

In an elegant paper, Sir Peter Medawar convincingly argued that one does not prove a hypothesis of the stature of evolution. On the other hand, he stated that there are abundant direct proofs of the plausability that evolution has occurred and is still occurring. Anyone who is worried about the quality of evidence for evolution will want to read this essay.

Edward O. Wilson praised Darwin as an unusual thinker and suggested that patterns of social behavior possess a biological basis shaped in large measure by natural selection, an idea supported to a considerable degree by Darwin. Wilson explained that Darwin's theory was greatly threatened by social insect groups. To Darwin, the question of how such systems could evolve when the worker castes leave no offspring "appeared insuperable, and actually fatal to my whole theory." Darwin remembered that selection may be applied to the family, as well as the individual, and thus anticipated the modern principle of kin selection. Those interested in sociobiology and/or gene-culture coevolution will find that this paper relates these subjects solidly within the framework of evolutionary biology.

In the final lecture, Jaroslav Pelikan departed from the particulars of Darwinian thought and reminded us that there were other ideas developing in nineteenth-century England. His paper, "Darwin's Legacy: Emanation, Evolution, and Development," examined what he calls "the evolution of evolution." In sprightly prose, he roamed from the earliest use of "evolution" by the seventeenth-century English Platonists to the acknowledgement of doctrinal development by John Henry Newman.

The readers will also enjoy the additional comments of Sir Peter and Professor Gould on *evolution* as a plastic term. These gems are among the many to be found in the section entitled "Conversations at Nobel XVIII," which follows the lecture texts.

Contributors

STEPHEN JAY GOULD
Professor of Geology, Harvard University; Curator of Invertebrate Paleontology, Museum of Comparative Zoology; Schuchert Award, 1975; president, American Society of Naturalists, 1979–80; American Book Award, Science, 1981; McArthur Foundation Prize Fellowship, 1981–86. Author of *Ever Since Darwin* (1977), *The Panda's Thumb* (1980), and *The Mismeasurement of Man* (1981); columnist for *Natural History* magazine.

IRVING STONE
Author whose biographies of Charles Darwin and Clarence Darrow are pertinent to the 1982 Nobel Conference topic. Rupert Holmes Award, 1961; Golden Plate Award, American Academy of Achievement, 1971; Cal-Berkeley Alumnus of the Year, 1971; Author of the Year Award, Book Bank USA, 1976. Author of *Lust for Life* (1934), *Sailor on Horseback* (1938), *Clarence Darrow for the Defense* (1941), *They Also Ran* (1943), *Adversary in the House* (1947), *Men to Match My Mountains* (1956), *The Agony and the Ecstasy* (1961), *Those Who Love* (1965), *The Passions of the Mind* (1971), and *The Origin* (1980, biography of Charles Darwin).

RICHARD E. LEAKEY
Director and Chief Executive, National Museums of Kenya; co-leader of paleontological expeditions to Lake Natron

(1963–64), Lake Baringo (1966), and Omo River (1967); leader of East Turkana Reserve Project (1968). Author of *Origins* (1978, with Roger Lewin), *People of the Lake* (1979, with Roger Lewin), and *The Making of Mankind* (1981).

Sir Peter B. Medawar

Professor of Experimental Medicine, Royal Institution; member of the Medical Research Council external staff, Transplantation Biology Section, Clinical Research Center, Middlesex, England: fellow, Royal Society, 1949; Commander, OBE, 1958; Royal Medal of the Royal Society, 1959; Nobel Prize in Medicine, 1960; knighted, 1965; Copley Medal of the Royal Society, 1969; Companion of Honour, 1972; Order of Merit, 1981. Author of *The Uniqueness of the Individual* (1957), *The Future of Man* (1960), *The Hope of Progress* (1972), *The Life of Science* (1977, text, with J. S. Medawar), and *Advice to a Young Scientist* (1979).

Edward O. Wilson

Baird Professor of Science, Harvard University; Curator of Entomology, Museum of Comparative Zoology. National Academy of Sciences; American Academy of Arts and Sciences; Mercer Award, Ecological Society of America, 1971; Distinguished Service Award, American Institute of Biological Sciences, 1976; National Medal of Science, 1977; Pulitzer Prize for General Non fiction, 1979; Leidy Medal, Academy of Natural Sciences, 1979. Author of *The Insect Societies* (1971), *Sociobiology: The New Synthesis* (1975), *On Human Nature* (1978), *Genes, Mind, and Culture* (1981, with C. J. Lumsden), and over 200 technical papers.

Jaroslav Pelikan

Sterling Professor of History, Yale University, Phi Beta Kappa (hon.), 1966; American Academy of Arts and Sciences, 1966 (vice-president 1976–79); Senior Fellow, NEH, 1967–68; National Award, World Slovak Congress, 1973; Christian Unity

Award from the Atonement Friars, 1975; Professional Achievement Award, University of Chicago Alumni Association, 1980. Author of *From Luther to Kierkegaard* (1950), *Fools for Christ* (1955), *The Shape of Death* (1961), *The Christian Intellectual* (1966), and *Historical Theology* (1971); editor for Encyclopedia Britannica, Luther's Works (22 volumes), 1955–70, and Twentieth Century Theology in the Making (3 volumes).

In Praise of Charles Darwin*

STEPHEN JAY GOULD

As if to provide future revelers with a double excuse for re-joicing, Charles Darwin was kind enough to publish his great work, *On the Origin of Species,* when he was exactly fifty years old. In 1959, we could celebrate both the centennial of his book and the sesquicentennial of his birth. And celebrate we did, with symposia and conferences throughout the world.

The only sour notes amidst all this merriment were sounded by scholars who followed a tradition, then prevalent, of labeling Darwin an anomaly in the history of ideas. He was, they said, a slow man of ordinary skills who happened to be in the right place at the right time; zeal and patience were the only virtues they acknowledged. One well-known biographer described Darwin as "limited intellectually and insensitive culturally"; another judged him "a great assembler of facts and a poor joiner of ideas . . . a man who does not belong with the great thinkers."

The 1959 celebrations inspired a wave of Darwinian scholarship that put these deprecating interpretations firmly to rest and elucidated the different but genuine nature of Darwin's

* This essay appeared originally in the February 1982 issue of *Discover* magazine. Excerpts from Stephen Jay Gould's extemporaneous talk at the 1982 Nobel Conference can be found in Appendix A of this book.

genius. Thus, as the next great excuse for a celebration arises —Darwin died one hundred years ago this April [1982], and we must mark deaths as well as births in our uncertain world —we see a different Darwin, a much more powerful and admirable man.

Darwin has been the inspiration of my life and work, joining my father and Joe DiMaggio in the select trio of men who most profoundly influenced my life. For the centennial of his death, I write this appreciation—a frankly celebratory essay, but an honest one. Let us rejoice that we can identify, in our complex and ambiguous world, a man with such power of thought and such influence upon us all—a man who, at the same time, managed to be an exemplary human being.

Darwin was born in Shrewsbury in 1809, on the very day that witnessed the birth of Abraham Lincoln. He had all the advantages that social class and money could offer. His father was a wealthy physician, his grandfather Erasmus Darwin, a celebrated writer whose books about nature, in heroic couplets, are often (and mistakenly) read as harbingers of his grandson's views. He was an indifferent student at Cambridge, primarily because of a lack of commitment. But Darwin suffered a sea change aboard the *Beagle* and returned, after five years of traveling around the globe, a confirmed naturalist, having abandoned his earlier plans to become a country parson. According to popular legend, the finches and tortoises of the Galapagos pushed Darwin over the edge to heresy. In fact, they (and other observations he made while aboard the *Beagle*) only nudged him in that direction; two years of concentrated effort in London after the voyage fueled his transition. He arranged his notes, read voraciously in all fields of science, poetry, and philosophy, filled notebook after notebook with telegraphic insights, and finally, in 1838, put it all together in the theory of natural selection.

About the externals of the rest of his life, we can say rather little of conventional interest. He married his cousin Emma

Wedgwood and lived a long and happy life with her, untouched by the slightest breath of poverty or scandal. He never again left the British Isles, and rarely even ventured forth from his country house at Downe, on the outskirts of London. His tragedies were those of all his contemporaries—the early deaths of several beloved children. His daily trials were retching and flatulence—a chronic illness of unknown cause that has provided endless (and largely fruitless) debate among Darwinian scholars.

But ah, consider the turmoil within his mind! For thirty years, he sat at Downe, turning out book after book, some disarmingly obscure (including tomes on climbing plants, orchids, and the formation of vegetable mold by earthworms), but all part and parcel of a general theory and approach that revolutionized human thought. Few men have influenced the world so profoundly and from such a citadel of apparent calm.

Why did Darwin, rather than Jean Baptiste Lamarck or Robert Chambers or any of the numerous evolutionists who preceded or followed him during the nineteenth century, become such a symbol and prime mover of the greatest transition in the history of biological thought? Scientists and historians have pondered this riddle for a century and have not resolved it thoroughly (thereby leaving enough work for the bicentennial in 2009). The points that seem important to me can be arranged in five categories, providing a framework for this appreciation.

The usable character of Darwin's theory. Darwin's fame cannot lie merely in the fact of his evolutionary convictions, for he had several predecessors among the greatest scientists of Europe (Lamarck and Geoffroy de Saint-Hilaire in France, in particular). But these predecessors had developed speculative theories, largely devoid of direct evidence and not subject to fruitful testing. Science can only traffic in usable and operational ideas.

On the Origin of Species provides copious evidence and direct suggestions for research, not merely a cosmic, untestable view suited more for contemplation in awe (or disgust) than for immediate use, scrutiny, and extension. Darwin, for the first time, gave scientists something practical to do.

Lamarck's theory had proposed an inherent force that "tends incessantly to complicate organization." He contrasted this internal perfecting tendency with the "influence of circumstances," or what we could today call adaptation to local environment. For Lamarck, small changes that could be observed and manipulated were not the substance of evolution's most important process—the drive toward perfection—but only tangential deflections that adapted creatures to local circumstances.

In Darwin's theory of natural selection, on the other hand, these small changes *are,* by extension, all of evolution. Darwin dispenses with unknown internal forces and attempts to render all change on all scales as the accumulated product of small and observable modifications. Thus, the breeding of pigeons and minor geographic variation within natural species become the stuff of all evolution. In studying what can be observed and measured, scientists examine the essence of the process, not merely a deflecting force opposed to an unknown internal drive. Darwin made evolution a *workable* science. From a professional's standpoint, there can be no greater praise. (I myself believe that Darwin went too far in attempting to reduce all large-scale phenomena to the gradual accumulation of small changes under natural selection. But this is a subject for another time, and my major point is only further confirmed: if Darwin had not established a *workable* theory of evolution, we would still be spinning stories in armchairs or over cocktails, not developing testable critiques.)

The radical implications of natural selection. The common denominator of the evolutionary theories proposed by Darwin's rivals lies in their congeniality with many traditional biases of Western thought that Darwin was trying to challenge or strip away. They view evolution as a foreordained process ruled by principles of inherent progress.

Natural selection, however, is a theory of local adaptation only. Changes that, in our anthropocentric way, we choose to call progressive represent only one pathway of adaptation to changing local environments. Every large-brained mammal harbors species of parasites so morphologically "degenerate" that they are little more than bags of reproductive tissue. Yet who can say that one or the other is "better" or any surer of evolutionary persistence?

If a denial of inherent progress were not radical enough, Darwin also introduced the specter of randomness into evolutionary theory. To be sure, randomness only provides a source of *variation* in Darwin's theory. Natural selection (a deterministic process) then scrutinizes the spectrum of random variants and preserves those individuals best adapted to changing local environments. Still, chance in any form was anathema to many nineteenth-century thinkers, both then and now.

Darwin's theory also challenged the comforting assumption that evolution must be purposive, working toward the good of species or ecosystems. The theory of natural selection, established in perhaps unconscious analogy to the individualistic, laissez-faire economics of Adam Smith (whom Darwin had been studying intensely just before he formulated his theory), speaks only of individuals struggling for personal success. In modern terms, natural selection concerns the unconscious struggle of individuals to leave more of their genes in surviving offspring. Any benefits to species, any harmony in ecosystems, arise merely as a by-product of this struggle among individuals or, in the case of ecosystems, as a natural balance among competitors.

What then of spirit, of vital forces, of God himself? No intervening spirit watches lovingly over the affairs of nature (though Newton's clock-winding god might have set up the machinery at the beginning of time and then let it run). No vital forces propel evolutionary change. And whatever we may think of God, his existence is not manifest in the products of nature.

Darwin was not an atheist. He probably retained a belief in some kind of personal god—but he did not grant his deity a directly and continuously intervening role in the evolutionary process. Many have viewed this message as pessimistic, or even nihilistic. I have always understood it (as I believe Darwin intended) as positive and exhilarating. It teaches us that the meaning of our lives cannot be read passively from the works of nature, but that we must struggle, think, and construct that meaning for ourselves. Moreover, Darwin maintained deep humility before the difficulty of such a task. He understood the limits of science.

The universal scope of Darwin's vision. Many of Darwin's fellow evolutionists, either through lack of courage or adherence to tradition, constructed tortured arguments to exclude human beings from their system and to make a divine exception for this one peculiar primate. Darwin persevered and built a general theory applicable to all organisms. We can, I believe, discern a trilogy of increasing daring among his major works. He published *The Origin of Species* and established his general theory in 1859. Of our species, he said only: "Light will be thrown on the origin of man and his history"; subsequent editions ventured the slightly intensified "much light." In 1871, he published *The Descent of Man* and argued that our bodies had also been molded by the forces of natural selection. Finally, in *The Expression of the Emotions in Man and Animals* (1872), he dared claim that our most refined and most particularly human behavior—the expression of our emotions—also reflected an evolutionary past. We express disgust with a facial motion associated with the adaptive act of vomiting. We curl our lips in rage, raising them most just where our useless canine teeth protrude; yet in our ancestors, these very teeth were long and sharp weapons. In our soul as well as our body, we display "the humble stamp of a lowly origin."

The consistency and depth of Darwin's thought.
Charles Darwin wrote fifteen books (excluding four monographs on the taxonomy of barnacles and his contribution to
Captain Fitzroy's narrative of the *Beagle's* voyage). Traditionally, these books were regarded as a motley collection—a few
revolutionary tomes to be sure, but mostly the trivial play-
things of a doddering naturalist. How else to view a book on
"the structure and distribution of coral reefs," or "on the
various contrivances by means of which orchids are fertilized
by insects," or on "the formation of vegetable mould, through
the action of worms"?

I think Darwinian scholars would not agree, however, that
the entire corpus of his work is one consistent, ramifying, and
remarkable exploration of his new view of life and its consequences. All his books are either about evolution or about the
extension to other subjects of his evolutionary method (the
study of historical continuity and the criteria for inferring
genealogical connection). His theory of coral reefs, for example, depends upon a recognition that all the varied forms of
modern reefs can be understood as stages of a single historical
sequence (continued upgrowth of reefs as supporting islands
sink below the sea). This theory, strongly challenged in Darwin's time, is now abundantly affirmed; the method of argument is identical with the inference of evolution from different stages in the process of speciation displayed by modern
populations.

The orchid book is not a compendium of a hobbist's minu-
tiae, but a long argument about why the imperfection of organic design illustrates evolutionary descent. When environments change, organisms must modify ancestral parts for new
functions. This legacy of the past precludes the development
of optimum designs. Orchids entice insects by modifying the
ordinary parts of flowers for new roles. The worm book treats
Darwin's favorite evolutionary theme: that an accumulation
of small changes produces large effects in the long run.

Darwin also recognized the profound and tumultuous effect

that evolution would work upon other traditional disciplines far from science. In a remarkable passage from an early note-book, for example, Darwin cuts through two thousand years of philosophical tradition with a single phrase: "Plato says in *Phaedo* that our imaginary ideas arise from the pre-existence of the soul, are not derivable from experience—read monkey for pre-existence."

True heroes must be made of flesh and blood. Had Darwin been a cold fish, or a nasty, exploitative man, we might be less attracted to him, though we would still admire the power of his thought. Yet he was a person whose basic kind-ness and decency defy the numerous attempts of detractors to demean or defame him. The external calm of his life belied an inner turmoil, but Darwin suppressed his anxieties, or chan-neled them into illness or work (depending upon your prefer-ence in psychoanalytic theories), and remained a truly emi-nent Victorian.

Darwin wins us, first of all, by his fine writing. He was not, as were the scientists Thomas Henry Huxley and Charles Lyell, a powerful and elegant stylist. He often wrote pages of adequate, but ordinary, descriptive prose. But he had a flair for metaphor and occasional outbursts of controlled passion. And these gems shine all the more because they are embedded in ordinary prose and we meet them unexpectedly, with delight. Consider his metaphors of the wedge, the tangled bank, the tree of life, or my favorite (in drawing a contrast between the superficial harmony of ecosystems and the underlying strug-gle for existence among individuals): "We behold the face of nature bright with gladness. . . ."

When Darwin uses this power of prose to advance social positions that most of us view as enlightened (Darwin was, in nineteenth-century parlance, a liberal committed to the abol-ishment of restraints upon the expression of human potential), the effect can be stunning. Consider this passage on slavery from the conclusion of his *Voyage of the Beagle:*

Near Rio de Janeiro I lived opposite to an old lady, who kept screws to crush the fingers of her female slaves. I have stayed in a house where a young household mulatto, daily and hourly, was reviled, beaten, and persecuted enough to break the spirit of the lowest animal. I have seen a little boy, six or seven years old, struck thrice with a horse-whip (before I could interfere) on his naked head, for having handed me a glass of water not quite clean. . . . And these deeds are done and palliated by men, who profess to love their neighbors as themselves, who believe in God, and pray that his Will be done on earth! It makes one's blood boil, yet heart tremble, to think that we Englishmen and our American descendants, with their boastful cry of liberty, have been and are so guilty.

Yet I do not wish to portray Darwin as a man of cardboard, for then he would be dull in his one-dimensionality, however admirable. Darwin had faults aplenty, even if most were the common attitudes of his age. Don't think that his many favorable words about blacks reflect a general egalitarian perspective. Virtually no white male of that era—neither Franklin, nor Jefferson, nor Lincoln—doubted the innate superiority of his race. Darwin spoke well of blacks because he had respect for this race as well, but read his words about the people of Tierra del Fuego if you wish to encounter the conventional intolerance of his age. As for women, his kindness includes little evidence of respect for their intellectual potential. In one particularly chilling, though uncharacteristic, private jotting, he had this to say about the advantages of marrying: "Constant companion (friend in old age) who will feel interested in one, object to be beloved and played with—better than a dog anyhow—Home and someone to take care of house—Charms of music and female chit-chat. These things good for one's health."

Darwin's humanity, with all its foibles, shines through in his life and writing. We can feel the pain of his inner conflict when, after working for twenty years on the theory of natural selection, he receives a short note from the English naturalist

Alfred Russel Wallace containing the identical theory devised one night during a malarial fit. Can he publish and preserve his legitimate priority, or must he stand aside? Gutsy humanity or abstract virtue? He writes to Lyell, exhorting him between the lines to find an honorable yet advantageous way: "I should be extremely glad now to publish a sketch of my general views . . . but I cannot persuade myself that I can do so honorably. . . . I would far rather burn my whole book, than that [Wallace] or any other man should think that I behaved in a paltry spirit. . . . My good dear friend, forgive me. This is a trumpery letter, influenced by trumpery feelings." (Lyell and other friends took the hint and arranged to publish Wallace's note along with parts of a sketch that Darwin had written during the 1840s. Author Arnold Brackman has recently suggested that Darwin actually cribbed parts of his theory from Wallace, but details of dates and places invalidate the claim.)

In any case, this debate only concerns a subsidiary issue called the principle of divergence. Priority for natural selection —the essence of the theory—cannot be denied to Darwin. He developed the idea in 1838, when Wallace was a teenager. In this, as in so many other incidents of Darwin's life, we understand in the most direct and poignant manner that science is, quintessentially, a human endeavor. Let us praise famous men for this fundamental lesson.

Darwin died in April 1882. He wished to be buried in his beloved village, but the sentiment of educated men demanded a place in Westminster Abbey beside Isaac Newton. As his coffin entered the vast building, the choir sang an anthem composed for the occasion. Its text, from the Book of Proverbs, may stand as the most fitting testimony to Darwin's greatness: "Happy is the man that findeth wisdom, and getteth understanding. She is more precious than rubies, and all the things thou canst desire are not to be compared unto her."

The Human Mind After Darwin

IRVING STONE

We are celebrating in this year of 1982 the centennial of Charles Darwin's death. Darwin's impact, along with that of Albert Einstein, Karl Marx, and Sigmund Freud, has been a dominating one of this hundred-year time span.

Our purpose is to take a brief look at the human mind since Darwin, a century of magnificent accomplishment and dismal failure. It is a good time to take such a discerning look, for that century has now come to climactic close. A new century of trial and error on the part of the collective mind is about to begin. Ten or fifteen years ago, there was hope that our "century of mismatch," as it has been called, might through intelligence resolve the problems arising from the onrushing technologies.

Today, in spite of the fact that the human is the single most brilliant, creative instrument developed on this earth, we have to admit that it has failed to find a human resolution for the peoples of our world. What was the human mind prior to Charles Darwin's body of work? What basic changes in the thought processes of that mind did his books bring about? With what accomplishments can we accredit him? What is the content and the method of the working mind today, and what can we expect from the future?

I do not refer to the anatomical or the physiological structure of the brain nor its relation to the nervous system. Rather I'm considering the mind first as a content and then as a system of acquiring that content and the using of it for individual or societal purposes. Before Darwin, the human mind was encased in a series of cells to which the keys had been thrown away. There was no such phenomenon as the right to know.

Illiteracy started at a 90 percent level under the Czars and came down slowly, if at all, as one moved through Europe. In England, which already had the Magna Charta, there was no education for the working classes until Thomas Huxley, known as Darwin's bulldog, began giving those classes himself and Alfred Russel Wallace, the first to corroborate Darwin's theory of natural selection, published fruitfully on the educational needs of the poor. The privileged percentile of the British who might secure an education were rigidly controlled in what they might study.

There existed no right to question. To question was anathema. When Darwin entered Christ College at Cambridge in 1828, there were few science courses. Science was anti-Scripture. A tiny group of adventuresome men, later Charles Darwin's mentors, had begun to lecture in the natural sciences— John Henslow on botany, Adam Sedgwick on geology. But they were obliged to form a group outside the university to discuss its broader scope under the name of philosophy. It was an age of the closed mind, the barred vision of the universe. It was unlawful to probe, to analyze, to ponder, to deduce, to think in new directions. The human mind was, in effect, the walnut which the brain has been said to resemble in appearance. A walnut encased in a hard shell.

It took Darwin's enormous talent to observe, his deductive skills, and his courage to record his findings to break open that shell. For those who were allowed an education, there were great riches. The poetry of Chaucer, Dante, Pushkin. The dramatic literature of Shakespeare, Racine, Molière. The paintings of Leonardo and Raphael. The sculpture of Michelangelo and Donatello. The music of Bach and Beethoven. The architecture of the Greeks or of Brunelleschi and Sir Christopher Wren. The science of Euclid, Copernicus, and Galileo. Fruits of the creative mind enriching life for those to whom it was available.

For the rest, individuals could be trained by practical experience, become expert in a craft; otherwise, the mind as it was born was the same mind that died years later. All wondering and learning of a systematic nature about the origin of our earth and the evolution of its varieties and species had been closed down by Archbishop James Usher in the mid-seventeenth century when he declared, "This world was created in the year 4,004 B.C. at nine o'clock in the morning."

When Charles Darwin grew up and attended Cambridge, this belief was promulgated by the Church of England. Ancient fossils discovered in mountain stratas, in deserts, on the shores of dried lakes or long-ago ocean beaches were met with the explanation that the great flood had deposited its effluvia in strange places. The limitless specimens of insects, plant, and beast were declared to have been individually and spontaneously created by God.

In the natural sciences, almost all discovery has served mankind well. Where there is a concerted search for truth, erroneous observation and deduction will inevitably creep in. Can it be said, then, that truth in art or science is a pursuit and not an achievable end? It certainly can be said that during this epic the human brain was held in slavery. The content of the mind became entrapped by the denial of the tools of learning, the instruments with which to broaden its scope of knowledge by this all pervading hagiocracy.

How did Charles Darwin open the human mind? What did

his life work accomplish? Perhaps above all he gave us a method of seeing and learning, an entrance to a vast and exciting new area of thought. His efforts have to be divided into these two parts: first, the modus and the tools for thinking which he provided us; and second, the astonishing content, not unlike the riches unveiled by Howard Carter's opening of Tutankhamen's tomb.

Under method, we have comparison, such as the beaks of the four finches from the neighboring islands of the Galápagos, comprehension, and the ability to correlate the findings and reflect this relationship—their relationship, a detached observation without interference from prejudice or emotion, the habit of tough mental skepticism, documentation, all evidence to be triple cross-checked, curiosity, the investigation of phenomena to get at their basic nature, self-doubt, the need to get away from early training into the open fields of objective inquiry. The "nothing sacred," no holy icons, myths, dogmas to prevent penetration to observable evidence. Systemization, the tools used to relate the parts to the whole. Imaginative projection and logical deduction, casting the mind forward to conceive all possible interpretations. The promulgation of theories, extending one's mental faculties to envisage organic unity. The courage to reconnoiter in enemy territory, to plunge through unmapped jungles, to dare the storms of uncharted seas, to pioneer new areas of understanding. Organization, putting together the innumerable shards of collected data into an architectural structure. Design that makes the elements fit functionally into all others of space, time, and category. Building order out of chaos by analyzing and hand-tooling into a pattern the disparate parts of a tumultuous spectrum. Wrecking, tearing down the Great Wall of China, so that new concepts and attitudes may sweep across the land.

How well did Darwin's methods serve us? Let us turn to medical science, for the results here are revolutionary. Consider the daring experimentation of Pasteur and Koch in the discovery of bacterial causes and immunization of infectious diseases, which has almost totally obliterated tuberculosis. The observation of the heroic Semmelweis in wiping out puerperal childbirth fever; Fleming's brilliant deduction which brought us the whole spectrum of wonder drugs and antibiotics. Marie Curie, who reached out for the tool of radium as a treatment for cancer. Röentgen, who gave us the magnificent use of the X ray. Today's Olendorf, who developed the CAT scan which can reveal a disturbance anywhere in the body. And Moniz, whose concept of angiography reveals all of the blood vessels of the body and the brain. Freud, who divested himself of shibboleths and charted the unconscious mind. Mendel, who did so for the body's heritage. Watson and Crick, who advanced the concept of DNA, the foundation of genetic engineering, to modify the gene structure of plants, to improve their growth as a food supply, and to improve the health status of man by correcting genetic defects.

Before Darwin, the content of the human mind included a rich heritage in the arts of past civilizations. The cave paintings in Lascaux, the Sumerian stone carvings, the sculpture and pyramids of Egypt, the marbles of Phidias and Praxiteles of Greece, along with its Acropolis and its dramatists—Aeschylus, Euripides, Sophocles—and the laws of Solon. The artifacts and cave murals of the Etruscans; the engineering and literature of Rome—Horace, Pliny, Ovid. The exquisitely illuminated manuscripts and mystery plays of the Dark Ages. Paintings in the Italian Renaissance—Giotto and Cimabue, Botticelli and Titian. The Golden Doors of Ghiberti. From Spain, Velazquez, El Greco, and Goya. From Holland, Rembrandt and Frans Hals. In England, Constable and Turner. All of this, not a catalog, but a random citation of creative genius.

In the sciences, we also think of Ptolemy, Aristotle, Galileo, Humboldt, Lamarck. No one man frees the mind of its shackles. Yet in the nineteenth century, those shackles, heavily encrusted with barnacles, were shaken by Charles Darwin as leader and as symbol for the freedom of investigation. The powers he released were in the natural sciences, the life sciences. But once the new virus of freedom against public opposition was injected into the social corpus, it quickly infected all aspects of man's endeavor.

Now, what was the new content of the mind, what were the fresh mental concepts that Darwin provided? Let us take a sampling from his enormous body of published works which caused an upheaval in the Western world and, in later decades, the Orient as well. As a result of finding on the Island of San Iago, off the coast of Africa, a strata of calcareous material containing seashells high above the surrounding water, he theorized that volcanic action can raise land masses. On Rat Island, near the mouth of the Río de la Plata, he noticed a strange-looking animal and remarked, "At first sight, everyone would pronounce this to be a snake. But these two small hind legs, or rather fins, could mark the passage by which nature joins the lizards to the snakes."

In the cliffs of Punta Alta in present-day Argentina, and in the cliffs above Rio Uruguay, he discovered a rich find of fossil bones and teeth belonging to long-extinct antediluvian animals such as the *Megatherium*. He later realized that this was proof that some species had completely died out because they could not adapt to their changing environment.

In Tierra del Fuego, he made the observation that the wings of three different species of birds had been adapted to serve. The steamer bird used its wings as paddles, the penguin as fins, the ostrich as sails to fly in the breeze. On the Galápagos Islands, he was puzzled that each island had its own giant tortoise with a different shape and design of carapace, each adapted to its environment for its survival.

It was a short time after the return of H.M.S. *Beagle* that Darwin's thinking advanced to the point where he could write in his species notebook, "We have absolute knowledge that species die and others replace them." A few months later, he was able to supply a principle for how this happened: "the destruction of all the less hardy ones and the preservation of accidental hardy ones."

After experiencing a tremendous earthquake in Valdivia, Chile, and studying the geological results, he wrote in his notebook, "For the future when I see a geological section traversed by any number of fissures, I shall well understand the reason. The earth is a mere crust over a fluid, melted mass."

While on the Keeling Islands, he came up with the accurate theory of the growth of coral polyps and how coral islands were formed. It took him years of study to prove that barnacles made the material with which they attached themselves to boulders or to the hulls of ships out of their own unformed eggs.

To prove that plant life on remote islands was not the result of spontaneous generation or a disappeared connecting landmass, he soaked seeds in a salt-water solution, documenting that plant life reached those islands in the form of seeds transported in weed stuffs, rafts, debris, claws, or the bowels of long-flying birds. He demonstrated that each variety of orchid had developed its own basinlike structure containing its pollen, and that only one species of insect could get at its particular pollen to fertilize its own kind.

He learned that the ability of plants to climb was due to the spontaneous circulatory movement of their upper internodes. And he learned that one type of insect-eating plant had true digestive capacity. He began documenting the evolution of man and wrote, after years of intense study, "We thus learn that man is descended from a hairy quadruped furnished with a tail and pointed ears, probably arboreal in its habits, and an inhabitant of the old world—an ancient marsupial animal and this through a long line of diversified forms."

In the arts and the humanities, in the social sciences invented since his time, in political economy, sociology, community planning, the psychiatry of human relationships, Darwin's method of free investigation expanded all forms of endeavor. When we were young and naive, we believed in progress as a constant and uninterrupted movement forward for the betterment of mankind. Harsh experience has proved that this is not a valid concept. Our well-being moves in cycles. The optimists among us would describe this as the movement of a pendulum or a metronome. The pessimists would describe it as a clock with hands endlessly circling from noon to midnight.

It is interesting to take a look at the arts as they enter the second century after Darwin. Writing and the ability to speak organized language is probably *Homo sapiens'* most astonishing accomplishment. The majority of the literature, drama, and poetry in the century before Darwin was cloyingly sentimental, idealistically romantic, morally pure, and heavily censored. The horizon of that literature has been vastly expanded, sometimes to the extent of formlessness and dubious content. But the freedom has been there. No avenues were blocked. Writers could explore the deepest recesses of human endeavor to reflect their times.

We had the Freudian novels of the 1920s, the proletarian novels of the 1930s, the war novels of the 1940s, the groping novels of the 1950s, the protest novels of the 1960s, the self-purged novels of the 1970s, and now the political science fiction of the 1980s. It can be no coincidence that the revolution in painting and literature in France, and its philosophy as well, occurred after the publication of *The Origin of Species.*

In reaching out to new depths of human understanding, in addition to Baudelaire in poetry and Zola in the novel, we have the emergence of the young Impressionists: Monet, Pissaro, Cezanne, Whistler, Dégas, and Renoir who overthrew the static storytelling painting of the beaux-arts. If painting and sculpture, following Cubism through the various forms of abstraction, have fallen into nonhuman forms, we nevertheless have the magnificent emotional distortions of Picasso.

In music, we have come far past the supremely melodic composers, such as Tschaikovsky and Schubert, into Schönberg's twelve-tone system that created a new language of sound which most of us have not yet learned to speak. In electronic music, all sounds are produced by the use of circuitry and the manipulation of sound waves. We have lost the memory of melody. We should know in another hundred years if the sacrifice has been worthwhile.

Since Darwin, we have enjoyed a century of landmark technological advances that have resulted in no small part from his contribution of methodology and expanded freedom. In transportation, there is the internal combustion engine and Henry Ford's production line, the Wright brothers' airplane and the jet engine. In the field of energy, the nuclear reactor. In communications, Marconi's wireless and satellites. In the domain of electronics, Lee DeForest's first electronic tubes for radio, which lead to transistors to the incredible memory chip and the super high frequencies of microwaves. In aerospace, radar and lasers. In agriculture, there is McCormick's reaper. In the area of chemicals, a staggering variety of synthetic materials. And for information processing, the entire range of computer technology.

As a people, we have been brilliant enough to diagnose and publicize the fatal ills of our age. But we have not had the audacity to achieve a working cure for those ills. Thanks to television and its use for "votes for charisma," we can have increasingly poor and incompetent political figures. Children will spend fewer hours in the classrooms than in front of TV sets. Man's nuclear fission created the A-bomb, then the H-bomb, and there is now research underway for a Q-bomb, which will be a thousand times more destructively powerful and which could bring about the complete annihilation of our world and all of Darwin's species.

Are we using our highly advanced machinery or is it using us? In the year 2082, at the end of another hundred-year cycle, will we look back and find that we have brought technology and humanism into a good working partnership? Will our powers have been dispersed in the interest of the world population or will we still have pockets of deprivation and ignorance, conceptions of warlike solutions to international problems?

What precisely did Darwin change? He unbolted the heavily locked doors of our minds and let them stand open to the sunshine of free inquiry. He liberated us to investigate, to understand, and to embrace all forms of life. He did not collect complete evidence to prove his theories of evolution and the descent of man. Nor was his fossil record complete, a record which the geologists, archaeologists, and paleontologists of our time are filling in with gratifying persistence. It is not quite enough to say that God planted those fossils in the rocks and the sea to fool mankind into thinking that our world is more than nine thousand years old.

It has been claimed that for every poison, there is an antidote. But as Darwin so well learned, for every antidote, there spring up half a dozen poisons. The world of the free mind which he bequeathed us is today being attacked and eroded. We face, as a people and as a nation, a heavily financed and doggedly thought-out plan to turn Charles Darwin into a nonperson, to purge his accomplishments from the classrooms, the textbooks, the libraries, and all other means of communication. He has been denounced as an anti-Christ in a world where a tightly locked, rigid mind is considered the gateway to salvation. Our scientists, our sociologists, our educators struggle valiantly to keep the human mind open and resourceful. But in a decade or two, they may be overwhelmed and driven underground. There may descend upon us another Dark Age before another Charles Darwin comes along and leads the revolution back to reason and intellectual scope.

Freedom is a contagious disease. Artists, scientists, humanists are Typhoid Marys. The Black Plague of independent thought can spread like wildfire. The revolution in the modern architecture of Louis Sullivan and Frank Lloyd Wright in the United States, the Bahaus in Germany, is an outstanding example. Gone are the cupolas and gingerbread facades of the Victorian era. Steel and glass provide clean and uncluttered lines that let in light and air.

While Darwin suffered more abuse than anyone in English history, being called every foul name in the English language, his message of natural selection, of the evolution of all living things spread rapidly to Asa Gray in the United States, to Ernst Haeckel in Germany, to the naturalists of France, Russia, Italy. Some of his theories had to be revised and amplified, but not his method of work. The outstanding scientists of his day —Thomas Huxley, Charles Lyell, Joseph Hooker, Alfred Wallace—declared that he had the single greatest talent in the history of science.

Why? Because he believed in an unshackled mind. Because he believed that an unshackled mind working long and dedicatedly could unravel the secrets of the universe, that everything was findable, that there were no limits to what the mind, once free to explore, could discover, document, and relate to the body of already existing knowledge.

In conclusion, let us indulge ourselves in the glories of our minds' accomplishments. In printing and distribution, there have been such startling advances that our country and, in fact, Western Europe is now flooded with a plethora of books, journals, brochures, monographs, newspapers. There is material available for all to read, to enlarge the content of their minds and the logical mechanisms of their thinking. In the visual arts, we have increased the number of practitioners a thousandfold and have provided them with colorful new materials with which to work. Hardly a city of any size is without its museum, gallery, exhibitions. Where once the noble art of ballet was confined to the Bolshoi and the Sadler's-Wells, there are now well-trained ballet companies in almost every city. Music once confined to philharmonic or opera subscribers pours out dozens of daily concerts and over the radio and television to millions of listeners.

Medicine and now health sciences have increased man's years on this earth. Yet, contemplating the human mind today, we are both amazed by its powers and confounded by its lack of overall result. In considering our total society—and it is the mind that creates society, not the other way around—we have to acknowledge that neither technological invention nor the spread of the arts has brought about harmony and stability or enabled us to live in peace with ourselves or our neighbors. We have learned that the early Greeks were right in saying *anthropos politicus animus*—man is a political animal. Man is also a warlike creature.

At the present moment, there are at least a dozen national and civil wars being waged simultaneously. A number of first-rate minds put together the European Common Market, and after World War II, we established the United Nations. But neither the Common Market nor the U.N. has been able to help us avoid intermittent aggression and chaos.

One of our greatest accomplishments has been in the extended understanding of man through the social sciences. We know to an infinitely greater degree what motivates man's thinking, feeling, and action. These disciplines have afforded us partial control over human conduct, as well as a medical approach to irrational or destructive behavior. But these valuable tools have not enabled us to eliminate dictatorships, genocide, or the all-consuming belief in military action and the horrifying tragedies it causes. Nor has our knowledge enabled us to prevent internecine wars of religious, political, or ideological origin.

We have the weapons at hand to abolish destruction, if only we could persuade ourselves to use them. In the United States,

England, Western Europe, and parts of the Orient, we have superseded the absolute right of royalty with varying forms of democratic government. Through long, hard struggle, we have achieved what our minds taught us were the imperatives of viable government: universal suffrage, division of powers, the separation of church and state. Yet we have failed in our mind's ability to control instinctual drives, passions, the dictates of Jung's collective unconscious.

The relation of the human mind to our basic instincts is an open field of inquiry. At the very least it can be said that our apparatus of logical thought has not controlled greed, envy, fear, hate, fraud, lust, concupiscence, suppression which allows individuals, communities, and whole nations venially to encroach on the public good. Censorship in all fields of activity is one of the most lethal enemies of our commonwealth.

The tragedy of the human mind is that in every age it destroys its own civilization. It is essential to know what man has come from. Darwin opened the door of our minds to the freedom to find out. Now a hundred years later, our hard-core, right-wing extremists in both politics and religion are doing their best to slam that door shut and return our mentality to darkness and bigotry. The universities will not be exempt.

We must understand to what an extent the human mind can dislocate itself. Those same self-labeled creationists who are working to abolish Darwin's theories on evolution and natural selection from the textbooks and from the public schools would eliminate all science, even mathematics, which could be used to disprove their contention that mankind was created by a single act of God nine thousand years ago. Biology, paleontology, astronomy, anthropology, biochemistry, geophysics can prove the slow emergence of this universe. They must therefore be abolished as heretical because they allegedly dispute the literal truth of Genesis. The separation of church and state, which has safeguarded our people from the miseries and bondage of past centuries, is coming back.

Must we await the appearance of another Charles Darwin? Or shall each and every one of us take up the mantle and become a Darwin of the next century? We have the mind, the mental apparatus, to make secure our freedom now tottering on the brink of extremism. We have the mental facility to control chaos, to create an orderly, prosperous, and peaceful society.

The question for the next century is, Which way will we go? What the mind can envisage in terms of disruption and ruin, the mind can also counterthrust and demolish. Through resourcefulness and courage, we can realize the full genius of the human mentality. We can preserve it or lose it entirely. Jeremiah is still crying in the wilderness. The choice is ours.

African Origins: A Review of the Record

RICHARD LEAKEY

When Charles Darwin wrote *The Origin of Species,* there was scant paleoanthropological information, very few fossils had been found, the geology of the sites of discovery were poorly understood, the fossil evidence pertaining to our own specific evolution was hardly known at all, and the zoology and ecology with which we are all so familiar and which make up such an important component of understanding evolution were still very much in their scientific infancy. Things have changed tremendously since then. We now have, in Africa and elsewhere, a collection of fossil remains that require really very little help. They speak for themselves. We can demonstrate very clearly transitions and changes that have occurred, and we can point to a heritage of our own species that extends way back in time. Exactly how far we can take it is more difficult, because we are dealing with the inadequacies of definitions that we ourselves have created. One of the sadnesses I have is that so often when the general public hears about studies of human origins, they hear of it in the context of emotional arguments, personality cults, and personality assassination attempts. I think these studies are more important than that. I also believe that within the next decade the last remaining questions concerning our origin will be documented from the fossil record and it will then be possible, as it almost is now, to turn back and to look whence we came—to understand the why, the when, and the how of humanity.

Before we look at some of the fossil evidence and discuss some of its implications, I'd like to digress momentarily and touch on one or two of the issues that are perhaps beyond my own responsibility, but which I feel obliged to address on an occasion such as this. The obvious question, Why paleoanthropology? Is it worth doing? Is it important? Why study origins when there are perfectly good alternative explanations? I think the answer must be that if we are going to solve some of the problems of the world and look forward to the management of this planet on the basis that we are concerned with the survival of the species rather than the survival of a particular part of that species, then we need to understand fully that we *are* a species. We are a single species, and the things that differentiate one group from another, be they physical characteristics, or cultural characteristics, or a combination of both—these differences have reasonable explanations and have a reasonable place in human society and should not and must not continue to be used to divide. I believe a knowledge of self, in a species sense, is important, and I believe that with this knowledge many problems may have a possible solution. However, I am specifically concerned with the origins as represented by the fossil remains that have been found and can be studied in museums. There are other aspects of the study of origins—such as, the origin of human behavior. One very complex question concerns the place of cultural development and the significance of cultural development in terms of the future as well as the past. When did we become a warlike animal? *Are* we a warlike animal? Is this something that is innate or is this something that is learned? Do we control our destiny or is our destiny already programmed into our genes? These questions are important. They are important to explore and they are important to discuss in an open forum of this kind.

I believe that there are going to be some problems with looking at cultural evolution from a genetic point of view. And I think it is fair to say, here and now, that I would, in a different forum, like to have a lengthy discussion on that question. It is a fascinating topic and a topic that is really in its infancy, but I would like to make it clear that I see cultural evolution as a totally different phenomenon than the evolution I wish to talk about now—physical evolution.

Having said that, let me turn to some of the points that worry me. They worry me because we have all sorts of arguments raging at the moment in the field of paleontology and biology. One of our difficulties is definition. When we talk about man, what do we mean? Do we mean the male? The male and the female? Do we mean *Homo sapiens?* Do we mean, as some suggest, *Homo sapiens sapiens?* What arrogance! What do we mean by man? What do we mean by man and ape? What is an ape, if it's not a man? What is a man, if it's not an ape? All of these issues require qualification and definition if you are going to have a meaningful dialogue. Certainly we are unique, but our uniqueness is really not as spectacular as many of us want to believe. We have heard, and I fully agree, that it is totally wrong to think of evolution having occurred to produce us. That sort of arrogant mistake goes with our definition of ourselves, *Homo sapiens.* People have worried about evolution since Darwin proposed the idea. I think had Darwin explicitly stated that evolution applied to all but humans, there would have been a far greater acceptance in Victorian society in England and Europe in his day. Nevertheless, Darwin specifically included us, as he must have done. However, if you look at some of the literature that is still being portrayed by radicals and by organizations such as the scientific creationists movement, you are struck by the fact that people are most concerned that we are related to the chimpanzees and the gorillas. This is the anathema which causes us pain.

What is the difference between a human and a chimpanzee? Well, it's not very difficult to see some differences, but when you analyze them, many of these differences are not absolute. You can say that a chimpanzee is not intelligent, but what do we mean by "not intelligent"? There are people who have lobotomies and medical problems who are not intelligent either, but they remain people. Youngsters, children are not intelligent. Even some of our friends are not particularly intelligent, but they are still truly human. So what is the definition of intelligence? I think we've got to look at some more fundamental characteristics, and I believe the most important thing about humanity, and one which I would stress in my interpretation, is the fact that we are upright. We walk on two legs. Biologically, genetically, we are very, very similar to the chimpanzees and gorillas, but they walk on four legs and we walk on two. That transition from a quadraped to a biped happened at a certain moment in time, presumably as a result of some selective pressure that made bipedalism advantageous. When it happened, I don't know. But to me, that marks the first appearance of humanity on planet Earth. We know that for a long period of time there were bipedal apes who roamed Africa but who were apes in terms of their brain size or development. At some point, and I think we know approximately when, a population of those bipedal apes underwent further change that relates directly to us. Selection favored a trend towards greater intellectual skills. There was an enlargement of the brain in absolute terms, but more importantly, there was a change in the internal organization and structure of the brain. This to me is the second important part of this evolutionary process and it is only those two parts that I think are really of importance to our story.

I believe it would be much easier to go back to the original suggestion, which could be termed a cladist suggestion, that we include ourselves and the other apes in a single family and not separate us on a family level. Look at us instead as simply different or distinct genera within that particular group of animals. If that were done, I believe the attempts to understand the evolutionary past as seen by the fossil record would be much easier. Much of what I will say in the latter part of this talk will, in fact, reflect this cladist preference in terms of the taxonomical organization of my thinking.

The sorts of questions that are undoubtedly burning in many people's minds were really brought to a focus in my thinking just two days ago when an elderly gentleman from quite near here, who had obviously spent a good part of his life on a farm in the corn, rose in a period after my lecture and asked me whether I had ever in all my experience met a monkey that knew the meaning of sin. I realized the importance of that question to this gentleman. Sin is an important part of Western culture. Sin is an important mental concept that helps us guide ourselves and, through ourselves, society in a particular direction. But *sin* is really a human word for knowing wrong from right. I am quite sure that other animals, particularly a monkey or a chimpanzee or a gorilla, will in certain instances know that something is wrong in terms of the social norms of the particular society of which it is a part. However, the monkey hasn't the burden of knowing it is a sin, simply that it is wrong, and therein lies the other important part of our story. When did we develop a brain that had the capability of such abstract ideas as wrong is a sin? I don't believe we will ever find out by looking at fossils. Nor do I believe we will ever find out by looking at chimpanzees. I think we have got to accept that there are certain questions about our origins that we will never understand. But that's not a problem. Most of life we don't understand, and I don't think we necessarily have to believe that every question will have an answer that is available to us.

Now as Steve Gould has said, there could well have been a situation where, had there not been some extraordinary event, possibly a collision with another stellar body, there would have been no humans or primates on planet Earth. This is theoretically plausible, as it's plausible that in the future there may be no humans or primates on planet Earth. And in some ways one might argue that the world would have been a better place had we all been bipedal dinosaurs trotting around the primeval swamps and forests. In any event, I want to stress, again, that evolution is not here to produce us. We are fortunate to be here, and we have a tremendous responsibility to stay here, but more importantly, to allow other creatures that share our planet to stay with us.

I mentioned earlier my concern with definitions and a description of where my research is focused. I am concerned with a point in time, probably between twenty and thirty million years ago, which is, I believe, where the first split occurred between the very primitive monkeylike animals and the group that we call the anthropoids. The second important point, as I see it, is the moment when bipedalism was developed. We don't know why bipedalism occurred, but I think this origin of humans, the beginning of humanity, the development of the bipedal ape, was a reaction to environmental change, and I believe environmental change occurred in Africa some time between 15 and 10 million years before the present. It was at that time that this huge continent underwent some very significant changes. The earth's crust developed two large domes, domes of upwelling of the earth's surface resulting in mountain ranges, and their effect of uplift was to create totally new ecological habitats. Where before Africa had been flat across the equatorial zone, for the first time Africa had a topography that was sufficiently extreme to produce totally different weather patterns and totally different vegetation patterns.

About 9 million years ago in the fossil record in Africa, you get the first appearance of the real grazing animals, animals adapted to feed on grass. It is to a response to that grassland habitat that we owe our origins, I think, and it is that response which particularly concerns me at the moment to determine whether or not we can relate the beginnings of bipedalism to that event.

You should remember that in Africa all of the fossil sites are on the Eastern side of the continent. They are associated with the Rift Valley. My own work has been in Northeastern Africa, while the work of Don Johanson and some teams from Berkeley and France has taken place in the Horn of Africa and traditionally the work on human origins was done in Southern Africa. But these fossil sites were all located on that side of the continent which still today is typified by grassland and steppeland, unlike the western side of the continent which is characterized by rain forests and semijungle. The great apes, other than man, living in Africa today are confined to the western side of the continent. They have remained in the forests from which, presumably, our own ancestors originally ventured.

We have in East Africa sites that range from 20 million years, where we have the very primitive apes, the *Dryopithecines*, to between 17 and 30 million years, where we have a group of creatures that have been called *Kenyapithecus, Sivapithecus,* and *Ramapithecus.* We have for some time thought these creatures might be human ancestors, but probably, at least in terms of *Sivapithecus*, they are more related to the ancestry of the orangutang in the Far East.

Later in time, from 13 to 7 million years, we have sites in China, Greece, Pakistan, and a few in Africa, including a new site in Kenya, where we have found some of these advanced apes. Recently there was a new discovery, New Hominid 1982, which hasn't been named and which is quite unlike anything we have found before. Higher up in the sequence, we have a number of sites that span the period between 7 and 3 million years, and in that group of sites we have a lot of evidence, particularly in the latter 2 or 3 million years, for bipedal apes. By that time, humans were in Africa, humans in the definition of being bipedal apes. And then further on, we have a tremendous wealth of African sites where we begin to get the first indications of selection favoring an enlarged brain, greater intelligence, and the first stirrings of what you might call culture or technology. In the last million years, we have the final modification of the bipedal ape to a single species leading directly to ourselves today. Africa has this extraordinary geological record with fossils all the way through. We are not talking about two or three fossils as we used to do, we are talking about hundreds of fossils and the record is too complete to dismiss.

What we are concerned about now is, of course, the development of modern humans, creatures that stand up, that have technology, that have speech, that do things together, that possess all of those typically human characteristics. What we are trying to understand is where we came from, how we came to be what we are. We have enough fossils to look back and to reconstruct a lot about the physical shape of our ancestors who lived between the present and about 3 million years ago. The further back you go, the less complete the record. Nevertheless, the salient point, and the point that I would like to stress, is that although there were probably several different species or nonbreeding groups of bipedal apes over long periods of time, they all shared the basic characteristics of being upright and bipedal. The only way in which we can distinguish them today is on the basis of the morphology or shape of their heads (see Figure 1). There is a definite difference in the region of the skulls of *Australopithecus robustus, Australopithecus africanus,* and the large-brained form that we have attributed to *Homo erectus* or *Homo habilis.* I don't want to get too much into these Latin names, but I do want to stress that the distinction we make is really in the morphology of the skull and teeth rather than in the morphology of the rest of the skeleton. So

Figure 1: Homo erectus, Australopithecus robustus, and Australopithecus africanus skulls

while it may seem that we find nothing but skulls, in fact we do have other parts of the skeleton. However, we are more concerned with the skulls simply because they tell us more about what was going on.

Between 100 thousand and 150 thousand years ago and the present, we find the large-brained forms of bipedal ape. This is not a skull from Africa, but a skull from Greece (see Figure 2). The *Petrolona skull* from Greece serves as an example of that time frame. It is very similar to skulls of similar antiquity that have been found in Africa, in Asia, and in other parts of Europe. These are characterized by having a brain size upwards of 1,200 cubic centimeters, which, of course, is substantially and significantly larger than any of the other apes. We see an increase of brain size as we come forward in time. There are obviously problems with a continuing brain-size increase, and I simply say that in modern society, you mustn't think of those around you who have larger heads as being more evolved. It is a curious thing that the constant increase of brain size presented difficulties in that the larger the brain in adulthood, the larger the brain needs to be in infancy, and a large head is less easily passed through the birth canal of the mother. We have today a situation where human children are, in essence, born prematurely. As you all are aware, either from your own immediate experience or that of your relatives, a

Figure 2: Petrolona skull

human baby is a remarkably useless creature for a very long time indeed. Quite hopeless. But if human babies were born with more development, particularly in the head, they would have larger heads, and these larger heads wouldn't get through the birth canals of humans who need to walk on two legs. The wider the hips, the more difficulty a person has in walking.

Anyway, let's say that we do have essentially modern forms going back 100 to 150 thousand years. There is the question of whether we can take the fully modern human form, *Homo sapiens,* as having a single source, the result of a single speciation event, or whether we must begin to view *Homo sapiens* as an inevitable consequence of a genetic character or suite of genetic characters established long before, so that in *sapiens,* we are simply seeing a stage or a grade. This is a complex question and one on which I am still open, but I believe that in all probability we will eventually determine that *Homo sapiens* arose where there were populations of what we are presently calling a different species, *Homo erectus.* And I'm not suggesting multiple speciation events. I am simply talking about the effect that culture must have had in keeping contact between genetic and genetically related populations.

As you go back from fully modern forms, you come to forms rather like the skull we found in Kenya of what we call *Homo erectus* (see Figure 3). It's probably wrong to call it *erectus* in terms of its being a separate species, characterized by having a large brain in a size range that is well ahead of the other human apes or their contemporary bipeds. In *Homo erectus,* we see these very prominent brow ridges, like visors, and a much longer face than that of a modern human. As the brain grows bigger over time, the face tends to become smaller and tucked in. The absolute size of the *Homo erectus* adult head and the absolute size of a modern head is probably about the same. It's simply that the proportions have changed between the face and the jaw and the back part containing the brain. When you look at a modern human and compare it to *Homo erectus,* you can see that there are similarities, but also that there are differences, and the real difference relates to the increase in the brain size.

If we go back beyond a million and a half years, we lose the characteristic *erectus* form and come to a thing we've been calling *Homo habilis,* which occurs in various African sites at about 2 million years and which represents, at the moment, the first evidence we have for an increase in brain size (see Figure 4). It's not very significant in terms of its absolute size, but there are morphological distinctions between the brains of these sort of creatures and their contemporaries, the *Aus-*

Figure 3: Homo erectus

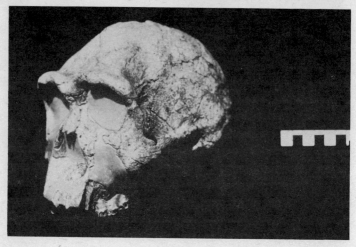

tralopithecines. It doesn't particularly matter to me whether you call it *Homo* or *Australopithecus* or *x* or *y*, it's simply important to note that there is a group of creatures that is distinct, that appears to change from this condition to the *Homo erectus* condition, and from the *Homo erectus* condition to the more modern *sapiens* condition. There does seem to be a progression. Now whether this is gradual change, or whether we can see moments of punctuation, is an open discussion at the moment. I am absolutely convinced that the initial shift, from a small ape-brain to a more advanced human-brain, was surely a punctuation and probably happened very rapidly. Once it happened, then the gradual refinement and development of that suite of characters could go on in a progressive and gradual way. Therefore, I would come down not in favor of Steve Gould's hypothesis or synthesis where we talk about evolution happening in fits and starts, nor would I come down in favor of the gradualistic approach, but rather I would suggest a little bit of both. Some things happen rapidly, while other things don't need to happen rapidly, but go on gently and in

Figure 4: Homo habilis

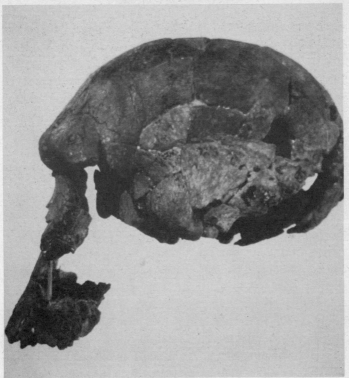

their own time, only accelerating or being cut off when environmental factors require it.

These are some of the theoretical arguments that we still have to consider. The archaeological record parallels the fossil record in the sense that from the first time we get large-brained forms, we also get the first evidence of stone implements, lithic industries, or culture. And there is a definite moment in time when we begin to see evidence of technology, which mirrors precisely the first evidence we have for a large brain.

If you had looked at *Homo erectus* a million and a half years ago, they almost certainly would have looked just like you and me from a distance. However, as you got closer, you would have noticed that their heads were the only part that made them different from us. A few years ago, I did a film series for BBC in which a group of actors simply wore face masks. The face masks were sufficiently well done that many people who saw the actors being prepared for filming, standing around, and smoking cigarettes didn't really catch on to the fact that they weren't rather odd modern humans. But then they realized that these actors had tremendous brow ridges and rather flat tops to their heads, and that led to questions as to where Leakey had picked up these odd people.

Now in addition to *Homo erectus,* or *Homo habilis,* we have contemporary with them groups of other bipedal apes, the *Australopithecines.* The *Australopithecines* were very successful in Africa, and again one must reflect that whereas the world could have been peopled or occupied solely by dinosaurs in their ascendency, it is also perfectly possible that the world could still have had *Australopithecines* rather than us. I am absolutely certain that the world would have been a better place, had the *Australopithecines* continued to rule the earth. We have all sorts of fragments of jaws and skulls in different stages. We even have the face of an *Australopithecine* with teeth beautifully preserved and also a youngish individual with the wisdom tooth still unerupted in the lower jaw.

The diversity of fossils suggests that there was more than one type of *Australopithecine.* There was a type that we call *Australopithecus africanus* that was contemporary with *Australopithecus robustus.* These strange creatures had absolutely no forehead and a huge, wide, and very flat face. These particular creatures were characterized by their dental adaptation, and they had very large molars and premolars which presumably were ideal for coping with a particular type of food. One can envisage an *Australopithecine* or *Australopithecus robustus* living out on the savannah where the food was not very nutritious and the only way to get enough energy was by eating a lot. If you are going to eat a lot of coarse food, you really need big teeth, otherwise they are just going to wear through. And so we see this as an adaptive suite in *Australopithecus robustus.* In our case, the adaptive suite was a larger brain.

Pressing on, I simply want to point out that in addition to jaws and teeth, we do have skeletons. The recent publicity given to a skeleton from Ethopia may have given some of you the impression that it is the only skeleton ever found. Lots of skeletons have been found, some more complete than others, but we have a very good idea about the bodies of our ancestors going back 1 to 3 million years. The other data we have are fossilized footprints. The earliest footprints of a bipedal ape ever found are dated at about 3.75 million years and were discovered by my mother in Tanzania (see Figure 5). There were three individuals who walked across the volcanic plain in which there had been a recent eruption of fresh ash, and they left behind their footprints, rather as if they had been walking down a sandy beach today. This is a remarkable monument to the antiquity of the bipedal ape. Certainly by 3.75 million years ago, there were bipeds on the African savannah. How much further back we can go is a moot point.

We have the *Ramapithecus* from Africa and from Asia, creatures represented really by teeth. One of the interesting things about *Ramapithecus* is that, for the first time, we begin to get evidence of an anthropoid, an ape with small canines. Now, the exact significance of that is not fully understood, but a lot of people have argued that if you are going to change your diet because you've changed your habitat, you are also going to need to change the way you deal with your food. In other words, if you are eating lush fruits in the forest, you can simply move your jaw up and down because the fruits will break up quite easily on your cuspid teeth. But if, instead, you are dealing with a food that may be drier and may be coming in smaller packages, it's quite useful to be able to prepare it

in your mouth by making a smaller bolus that you can swallow. In order to do that, you probably need to have more movement in your jaws, and in addition to being able to move them up and down, you need to move your jaws from side to side.

The *Ramapithecines* may well prove to be the ancestors to the Asian orangutang and a group of creatures that are now extinct. For a long time, we have thought of *Ramapithecines* as an ancestral hominid. I think we were wrong, and in view of the increasing body of evidence, it seems that we are simply dealing with an early orang. Interestingly enough, we can trace the origin of the orangs to Africa, and we have specimens from Lake Turkana that are widely known in the literature and are absolutely, unmistakably the ancestors to the orang-sivapithecus group. We have a number of specimens from this new site in Kenya that is yet to be fully worked, where we may be able to understand the origin of the Asiatic apes.

We know that about twenty million years ago, there was a rather poor-looking ape wandering around the forest of Africa from which all the later apes arose. These *Dryopithecines* can be considered ancestors to the apes and were probably fairly generalized chimpanzeelike forest dwellers. Skeletal evidence indicates that they were probably not knuckle walkers and could have been equally at home on the ground or in the trees. Their locomotor abilities may have been similar to modern monkeys. I think it's much easier to look at the *Dryopithescines* as ancestors to the apes and to look at ourselves as apes in the context of the evolutionary story that the fossil record can give us. If that is the case, the *Dryopithescines* would be one of those very early apes from which we ultimately can trace our own pedigree.

Traditionally, primates have been classified since just after the time of Linneaus, and as zoology advanced, the taxonomic arrangement became based on the geographic distribution of the primates. The Anthropoids now are divided into the *Pla-*

tyrrhines, or New World monkeys, and the *Catarrhines,* or Old World monkeys, which are confined to Asia and Africa today. Within this group, you have the Hominoidea broken into two families, the Pongidae and the Hominidae. This has been the standard classification and one which I think has worked perfectly well without the new data that we now have. Remember that charts, names, and relationships are devised by us; they are a construct of the human mind. We don't yet find fossils with labels attached to them telling us what they are. And this is a great problem because most of us are literate and we can read labels, but when we have to attach labels, we often use different labels for the same thing. I don't think there is anything sacrosanct about classification schemes, and I think it would be very useful to inject a new sense of adventure into some of the brighter and younger minds who would begin to ask questions as to whether or not by reorganizing things, we couldn't develop a clearer picture (see Figure 6).

I believe it might be useful to take the Hominoidea and to

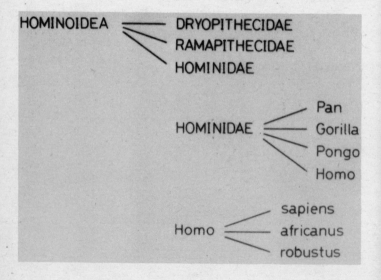

reorganize it in the following manner: place the *Dryopithescines,* the *Ramapithescines* and the fossil Hominoidea into an early Miocene group; then take the extant and recently extinct forms—including chimps, gorillas, orangs, and humans—into the family Hominidae as separate genera; and utilize *Homo* as the generic name for a bipedal ape. The first evidence of bipedalism would qualify for inclusion in the genus *Homo,* which would include *sapiens, africanus,* and *robustus.* The criteria for *sapiens* would be evidence of the enlargement of the brain. *Africanus* would include some of these rather strange things like *Australopithecus africanus,* and the small Australopithecine from the Hadar, "Lucy." A third species, *robustus,* would include the previously described large-toothed form. These would be true species that are, in fact, lineages that can be traced in the fossil record.

If we were to look at the fossil record in terms of *Homo sapiens,* the large-brained form, we could then divide the genus on a numerical basis as follows: the modern form or ourselves as Stage 5; what I've termed the Neanderthaloid form or the 100-thousand-year-old form as Stage 4; the erectuses, whether they are African or Asian, as Stage 3; *habilis* as Stage 2; and let's give ourselves a little opportunity for future glory by leaving Stage 1 still to be determined. By adopting a scheme like this, there is much more flexibility in dealing with the implications of speciation, the implications of isolated populations, and the effects of that on change. This is not a popular idea, and it has certainly not been accepted. I'm not absolutely sure that I accept it myself, but I thought it would be worth throwing out at a Nobel Conference to try and stimulate some discussion. I think it is important to devise some means by which we can talk to each other. And I think a large part of the problem in paleoanthropology is not that we haven't got the evidence, it's that we haven't got the vocabulary and we are depending on schemes that simply don't fit the modern pattern of knowledge.

We have now a considerable body of knowledge. There is no doubt at all that we have evolved. There is no doubt at all that our ancestors were not like us. There is no doubt at all that things such as culture, technology, language, art, and all that which makes up so much of our daily lives have developed over a very long time span. Some of them we will document. Some of them we won't. When did language begin? I don't know. I can tell you that skulls we have of *Homo erectus,* or Homo Stage 3, suggest that they had the morphological requirement for containing a brain that has motor areas developed for things such as speech, but this is different from saying that we *know* when speech began. It would be my view, however, that if you take the development of a large brain as the uniqueness of *Homo sapiens,* and if you accept that with a large brain, you are going to get technology, culture, and communication, then you are, in effect, from that moment putting us in a different position from other forms of life. I believe that if you allow culture to be part of the driving force of human evolution, then it's perfectly possible to have ourselves, *sapiens sapiens sapiens,* arising from populations of *Homo sapiens* that were less advanced in terms of their cranial development or brain development than we are today, without having to invoke parallel evolution or multiple speciation events which are unacceptable to me, as I think they are to many people.

The truth is, we simply don't have enough information to answer those questions. But the exciting thing is that, with the synthesis being made possible by new approaches, new studies, new techniques, and with the opportunity to think afresh, there is a very good chance that those questions will in fact be solved. I think it's tremendously exciting to recognize that in the very near future, we may finally be able to look at ourselves and know ourselves. I think it's worth carrying on with that task.

The Evidences of Evolution

SIR PETER MEDAWAR

I am about to address you on the subject of the evidences for evolution. Before I weigh in on that, I should like to say about Darwinism generally that it has had a great variety of vertiginous ups and downs in the past one hundred years. You know very well how, in 1860, the publication of *The Origin of Species* caused an uproar of resentment and disbelief of which the most prominent spokesman was that Bishop of Winchester, Samuel Wilberforce, whose promiscuous piety earned him the name of "Soapy Sam." Soapy Sam was he who was injudicious enough to tease Thomas Henry Huxley at the Oxford meeting of the British Association for the Advancement of Science. He was foolish enough to ask Thomas Henry Huxley on which side of his family he claimed to be descended from the apes, from his mother's side or his father's side? Now this was a singularly injudicious question, partly because it provoked a rebuke from Thomas Henry Huxley which caused Soapy to disappear promptly from history, and he is never thought of nowadays except as the butt of Thomas Henry Huxley. There are more serious reasons why he was injudicious. He could have taken the opportunity to inject a note of rational piety into the uproar about evolution that was in progress. He *could* have done that, but he missed his chance. Instead he inaugurated, single-handedly, the tension between religion and science. That is one of the disfigurements of the cultural history of the Western world. All this was quite unnecessary, simply because he didn't have enough character and sense to keep his mouth shut.

In the early years of the century, the mechanism of heredity of which Darwin had no conception at all, slowly began to be known because of the promulgation of Mendel's experiments and his findings by a number of students of heredity, especially William Bateson in England. From the standpoint of the man who knew something about heredity, Darwinism seemed very unsatisfactory. To him, it seemed altogether too glib and facile. William Bateson said of Darwinism, the discussion of anything to do with the origin of species nowadays is marked by "the apathy characteristic of an age of faith." Everyone believed Darwin had solved it all, but Bateson was very clear that he had not.

Then natural historians also get impatient with Darwin. D'Arcy Wentworth Thompson, a man whom we should now call a biophysicist, was trying to explain in physical and chemical terms how the skeletal spicules of sponges take the exact, intricate, and highly regular geometrical forms which they have. His attempt was unsuccessful, I regret to say. The only point I wish to make is that D'Arcy Thompson was not amused, and he held up to public obloquy the explanation of Professor E. A. Minchen, a contemporary professor of zoology, that the forms of spicules are the result of "adaptation to the requirements of the sponge as a whole, produced by the action of natural selection on variation in every direction." I say it again to bring out the full enormity of this statement: the shapes of these spicules are an adequately explained "adaptation to the requirements of the sponge as a whole, produced by the action of natural selection on variation in every direction." This glib formula annoyed D'Arcy

Thompson no end. There is no known biological situation for which that glib formula could not be applied. Natural historians in particular felt that this was simply not good enough.

For a variety of technical reasons which some of the speakers have hinted at, and I shall not go into them, Darwinism is still today under professional attack. And this has given rise to the misapprehension, shared apparently by all members of the lay public, that somehow the hypothesis of evolution has been discredited and creationism has been rehabilitated. These are misunderstandings which I will try to do my best to clarify.

The first misunderstanding is one which Steve Gould and Richard Leakey have already mentioned. That is the equation of Darwinism to the hypothesis of evolution. Many have done biology at school or done it here. And one lesson we were taught most emphatically is that Darwinism and the hypothesis of evolution are two very different things. Evolution is an historical statement about what is thought to have happened in the past. Darwinism is an attempted explanation of how evolution came about. If Darwinism is found wanting, this should not in any degree shake our confidence in evolution. Another cause for misunderstanding is the belief on the part of the lay public that one *proves* such hypotheses as the hypothesis of evolution. It is thought that there are a number of proofs, the acceptance of which justifies our believing in evolution. This is not the case. You may think that my using the term *hypothesis* is a symptom of my own uncertainty and a lack of deep conviction about the process of evolution. This is indeed not the case. A hypothesis is an imaginative preconception of what the truth *might* be. Every hypothesis is the invention of a possible world which may or may not be the real world. The word has no pejorative connotation. I must tell you with brutal frankness that it is a sign of philosophic illiteracy to suppose that the word *hypothesis* is pejorative in any sense whatsoever. The question then arises, How are hypotheses of the stature of evolution proved? The answer is that they are not proved. Hypotheses of the explanatories compass of, say, evolution or the Wegener hypothesis may or may not come to be accepted. But there's no logical process whatsoever by which they can be proved.

I may say I'm telling you dogmatically, because this is the view of all professional philosophers, including my own personal guru, Karl Popper. It was also the opinion of the leading American philosopher, as I believe him to be, Charles Saunders Peirce. He said, "The conclusions of science make no pretence to being more than probable." John Venn of Cambridge said, "no ultimate objective certainty . . . is attainable by any exercise of human reason."

The point is that there can logically be no proof of evolution that enjoys apodictic certainty. That is to say, there is no definitive proof so conclusive, so finally conclusive, that it leaves no possibility of criticism and, if necessary, modification. I must try and bring it home to you that the acceptance of the evolution hypothesis does not depend upon the testimony of proofs of any kind. The best thing to do is to give you a parallel. Consider the so-called proof of the hypothesis that the world is spherical. I can remember being told as a child that it was so. A likely story! I thought. And because there was a general susurration of skepticism among the little scholars, so we were presented with proofs of the roundness of the world. We were told, for example, that when a ship at sea hove into view over the horizon, one saw first its mast, its sails, its funnels and other superstructures. And only later did the hull come into view. Well, that's the proof. You see if the real world is round, that's just what one would expect. So we were fobbed off with such proofs of roundness of the earth. We didn't think it very convincing, although we were too naive at the time to say that this *is* a characteristic trick of refraction such as one might expect to find at horizon level, the kind of thing that gives rise to a mirage. Anyway, we were not very convinced. So we were told that if you set into the ground three poles or pylons of the same height and in a straight line, the one in the middle would look higher than the two at either end. This, again, didn't carry conviction, because we said, if one were to look higher, then obviously they weren't all three the same height. You would simply lower the one in the middle until it did look the same height as the others, so it's a somewhat reflexive proof.

We do not believe in the sphericality of the earth because of any particular proofs of it whatsoever. We believe it because the notion of the roundness of the earth underlies the whole of navigation. Marine navigation and aerial navigation. It underlies the whole of geodesy and the whole of chronometry, most of which would be unimaginable if you took the view that the world is flat. You could never seriously believe that astrophysicists heaved a great sigh of relief when satellite pictures of the world or pictures of the world taken from the moon showed it to be, well, not spherical for that matter—but rather an oblate spheroid. Which shows you shouldn't be too cocksure about anything.

In the same way, no believer in evolution such as Steve Gould and Richard Leakey and I ever heaved any sigh of relief when experimental simulations of evolution by plant and animal breeding demonstrated the inherent plausibility of the evolutionary transformation and also of selection as its agent. Most of the so-called proofs of evolution which are taught to schoolchildren and which are thought by the lay public to be proofs of evolution, and which they take pleasure in rebutting, are on the same level as those proofs of the roundness of the world. One of them you know—you must all have heard it—is based upon Haeckel's notion of recapitulation. It is usually summarized by saying that, in development, an organism "climbs up its own family tree." It recapitulates in its life history its own evolutionary history. Thus, human beings, we are told, go through a fishlike stage. Well, I didn't—and I don't suppose Steve Gould did either. There's no truth in the notion whatsoever. So opponents of evolution who set forth to demolish this argument are right to do so. But it has no effect on the acceptability of the notion of evolution.

There *is* an element of truth in the so-called law of recapitulation, and it's embodied in Von Baer's law. This affirms that the embryos and young of related animals resemble each other more closely than the adults into which they develop. As these embryos and youngsters grow up, they become more and more dissimilar, adopting eventually their adult specific forms. And this is how it comes about that human embryos are at some stage like fish embryos and very like reptilian embryos. Like fish embryos, human embryos have a pharynx, which is a great antechamber to the gut and perforated by apertures sometimes called gill slits. These apertures are the gill slits human beings were reputed to have. And human embryos, like all mammalian embryos, have a complete set of cellular envelopes and membranes for holding and processing yolk. Although the mammalian egg has no yolk, it has the same apparatus as the reptile's egg has for holding and processing yolk. Similarities between mammalian embryos generally and fish embryos in such things as the possession of yolk membranes by the human egg were thought by Thomas Hunt Morgan, and also Thomas Henry Huxley, to be evidence sufficient in itself to justify the acceptance of the evolutionary hypothesis.

So I must emphasize this point: the acceptance of the hypothesis of evolution does not depend upon proofs. We also recognize that there is in biology the equivalent of that direct evidence, that direct proof, that is akin to seeing the roundness of the earth in a satellite photograph. Because evolution has occurred quite recently—is still occurring. What has been described as the most notable evolutionary change that has occurred within our own lifetime is that in which melanism— that is, the evolution of smoky or dusky colored variants of moths and butterflies—has swept through industrial country-side where so much of the foliage is blackened by smoke and industrial effluents.

Then evolution is taking place briskly in many hospitals right now. Strains of staphylocci and streptococci are evolving rapidly towards resistance to the action of penicillin and many other antibiotics. This phenomenon has been seized upon by opponents of what they are pleased to think of as mechanized medicine as evidence that penicillin is greatly overrated, is losing its power. They don't realize that rather than penicillin losing its power, the bacteria are evolving into possession of a new power to metabolize penicillin and to be unaffected by it. Add to these the many other examples of evolution with which you are already familiar—such as the changes that have been brought about in domestic dogs, not by natural selection, but by artificial selection (probably the most powerful weapon of genetic engineering) and which have created breeds as different as Alsatians and Great Danes, on the one hand, and the little mutant horrors favored by fashion, on the other hand.

Now, these are direct proofs of the plausibility of evolution and of its having occurred. Whether we, through natural selection, are the agents or by whatever means. So why do we believe in evolution? We accept evolution because it alone makes sense of the great ladder of being, the great scale of being we have often referred to. Only the evolutionary hypothesis makes sense of the pattern of similarities and differences shown up by comparative anatomy and by the investigation of homologies. Only the evolution theory makes sense of vestigial organs. You all know that horses run around on their tippy toes, on the middle finger or the middle toe, respectively, of the fore feet and the hind feet—comparative anatomy taught us this about one hundred and fifty years ago. And the second and fourth fingers and toes are vestigial and remain as "splint bones." Well, evolution explains that, just as it explains such vestigial organs as yolk membranes in the embryos of mammals when the eggs of these animals have no yolks at all. It also explains, for example, the pineal organ. And only evolution adequately, plausibly, explains the existence of strange anomalous animals such as fish with lungs, which are common in Gondwanaland and therefore are still found in Australia, Africa, and South America. Then, how otherwise would you account for the existence of dinosaurs with feathers, mammals with flippers instead of feet, mammals that lay eggs? The evolutionary hypothesis encompasses all these phenomena and replaces, with one stroke of the pen, what would have to be a whole library of special pleading to account for how these animals exist.

These are the reasons why professionals believe in evolution. Misgivings about Darwinism itself are an entirely separate consideration. I answer most emphatically, and no amount of questioning will make me change this opinion, that the profession believes in evolution and that a professional biologist is an evolutionist. He realizes that the alternative to thinking in evolutionary terms about the subject matter of biology is to avoid thinking at all. That is a rather desperate expedient to which it seems the opponents of the hypothesis of evolution are ever more frequently having recourse.

Sociobiology: From Darwin to the Present

EDWARD O. WILSON

Sociobiology, contrary to a widespread popular impression, is not a particular theory of behavior—at least, not one that attempts to be more specific than the evolution of behavior by natural selection. It is a scientific discipline and, as such, is defined as the systematic study of the biological basis of social phenomena (including sexual and parental behavior) in all kinds of organisms, up to and including man. General sociobiology can be usefully distinguished from human sociobiology, the subdiscipline that addresses topics peculiar to man. Public interest and controversy has, of course, centered on human sociobiology, but most persons working on sociobiology are only marginally concerned with such matters. They are principally zoologists, students of animal behavior who specialize on various social animals from siphonophores to ants and chimpanzees.

Sociobiology is aligned with ethology, which can be defined loosely as the study of whole patterns of behavior under natural conditions (see, for example, the characterization by Thorpe, 1979). Both disciplines pay close attention to the evolutionary history of species and the manner in which behavior adapts organisms to their environment. But where ethology is centered in the details of individual behavior, including the activity of the nervous system and the effects of hormones, sociobiology concentrates on the more complex forms of social behavior, as well as the organization of entire societies. As a consequence, ethology consists to a substantial degree in the study of physiology and anatomy, while sociobiology is based principally on population biology—that is, the genetics, ecology, age structure, and other biological traits of whole aggregates of individuals.

Both ethology and sociobiology are concerned with "how" questions: how genes prescribe information, how the central nervous system mediates behavior, and so forth. They also address "why" questions: for example, why honeybee colonies divide at a certain time of the year and why parents behave altruistically toward their offspring.*The query "Why?" can be answered only by the study of history. And the history of biological process is, by definition, evolution. Its creative process is natural selection, the understanding of which is Charles Darwin's great legacy.

Evolution sometimes proceeds by means other than natural selection. Particular mutations may occur often enough to push up the frequency of the derivative alleles in the population without the aid of natural selection. Alternatively, immigrants can bring new genes into the population at a high enough rate to change the overall genetic composition of the population. Random drift can produce additional significant shifts in gene frequency. In the smallest populations, it undoubtedly leads to the total loss or fixation of some competing alleles. These auxiliary phenomena occur in nature and are unquestionably important under special circumstances, but

---

* The analysis of the function of both individual and social behavior in natural environments—in other words, the "why" aspect in the broadest sense—is often referred to as behavioral ecology. Clearly, the three disciplines —ethology, sociobiology, and behavioral ecology—overlap broadly, while emphasizing different levels of biological organization in the overall study of animal behavior.

most biologists agree that they are much less potent than natural selection in directing evolution over long periods of time. Left to themselves, they tend to lead to steady states in gene frequency. In other words, it is generally accepted that natural selection is the dominant mode of creative evolution.

Imperfections abound in this process. Not all biological phenomena are adaptive in each moment of time. Nonadaptive phenomena in social behavior and organization have been documented (Wilson, 1975a), and techniques have been devised to measure the degree of approach to local adaptive optima attained by insect societies (Oster and Wilson, 1978; Wilson, 1980). Nevertheless, as any field biologist can attest, a large part of behavior and social organization observed in free-ranging populations is demonstrably adaptive with reference to local environments, often in a close, detailed manner. The agency of natural selection should never be accepted in particular cases until proved, but it can always serve as a powerful and heuristic hypothesis. For biologists, as opposed to philosophers, this was Darwin's major contribution. "It is a revelation to the modern reader," Ernst Mayr (1964) concluded in his reintroduction to the first edition of *On the Origin of Species*,

how fully aware Darwin was that success in leaving progeny is a more important component of natural selection than is mere survival. His discussions make it abundantly clear that he considered selection not a purely negative force that eliminates the unfit, but a positive, constructive force that accumulates the beneficial. . . . He was also aware of the probabilistic character of natural selection: "Natural selection will not produce absolute perfection" [*Origin*, p. 202]. In retrospect, it is evident that nearly all the denunciations of Darwin's ideas on natural selection were based on an incomplete knowledge of the *Origin* and on misunderstanding.

And so it has been with a great deal of the criticism of sociobiology, insofar as that subject has been based upon the modern theory of natural selection. The proposition that patterns of social behavior possess a biological foundation shaped by natural selection, which was originated to a considerable extent by Darwin himself, does not imply that such patterns represent the best of all possible worlds. Even less does it imply that evolution of social behavior has ceased, or that all variation is necessarily adaptive and explainable by natural selection. Sociobiology is tied closely to general evolutionary biology, and its principles are evaluated with reference to that encompassing discipline.

Darwin's Contributions to Sociobiology

Darwin began his career as a naturalist with a passionate devotion to beetle collecting, and he maintained a lifelong interest in entomology. As the theory of natural selection took shape, he drew heavily on social phenomena for exemplification, both in favor of and (potentially) against his central argument. Darwin felt in particular that if he could accommodate various of the strange and complicated phenomena of the insect societies, evolution would be much more firmly entrenched. If he failed, the idea of universal evolution would be gravely endangered. Because Darwin attacked the problems head on and with considerable energy, the result was a set of remarkably modern conclusions.

The honeybee comb. "He must be a dull man who can examine the exquisite structure of the comb, so beautifully adapted to its end, without enthusiastic admiration" (*Origin,* p. 224). Darwin confirmed from the calculations of mathematicians that the hexagonal, contiguous, and thin-walled cells made by the honeybee workers are precisely the form needed to hold the maximum amount of honey. He supposed that this remarkable result could have arisen as the terminus of a short evolutionary series that can still be detected among the living species of social bees: beginning with abandoned silken cocoons used to hold honey, as in the bumblebees; then moving on to aggregates of spherical waxen receptacles, as assembled by the stingless meliponine bees, which also build the walls flat rather than curved when the receptacles are close enough to touch; and culminating with the method employed by honeybee workers, which construct their waxen cells as closely together as possible, so that all the walls are contiguous and flat. If you place a mass of equal-size spheres with flexible walls on a table and press them tightly together, the result will be a sheet of hexagonal columns—in other words, the honeycomb. Darwin saw no great difficulty in deriving this configuration stepwise from the relatively primitive food-storage behavior displayed in modern times by the bumblebees. Subsequent work on the sensory physiology of hive building, and its evolution within the hundreds of living species of social bees, has added large amounts of valuable information, but not challenged Darwin's interpretation in any significant detail (Lindauer, 1971; Michener, 1974).

Ant slavery. In the northern hemisphere are found ant species belonging to eight genera *(Leptothorax, Chalepoxenus, Epimyrma, Harpegoxenus, Strongylognathus, Formica, Polyergus, Rossomyrmex),* whose workers regularly raid the nests of other ant species, carry away pupae (individuals in the final, inert stage of development), and allow them to emerge as adults (Buschinger, 1981). The slave workers then accept the raiders as their sisters and proceed to care for them. They also attend to nest construction, foraging, brood care, and the other quotidian tasks of their instinctual repertory. Thanks to an earlier report by Pierre Huber (1810), Darwin was aware of the slave-making behavior of *Formica sanguinea,* a large red-and-black species that occurs widely in Europe, including southern England. He was understandably skeptical: "one may well be excused for doubting the truth of so extraordinary and odious an instinct as that of making slaves" *(Origin,* p. 220). But Darwin, the erstwhile entomologist, succeeded in confirming the phenomenon with studies around his own home at Downe. He excavated fourteen nests of *F. sanguinea* and found them all to contain slaves. He also witnessed a slave raid and colony emigration. He conjectured that the slave-making instinct might have originated from the far more widespread habit found in ants of capturing the larvae and pupae of other species for food: "It is possible that pupae originally stored as food might become developed; and the ants thus unintentionally reared would follow their proper instincts, and do what work they could." If the adventitious slaves then improved the survival and reproduction of the raiders, the predatory habit might be converted into a regular form of slave-raiding. Darwin was on the right track once again, but apparently not completely correct in his educated guess concerning the precondition. Recent research with the North American *Leptothorax duloticus,* which shows a primitive form of slave-making, suggests that territorial aggression, rather than predation, was the prime impetus. In conquering the nests of other members of the same and similar species, various *Leptothorax* species often appropriate part of the brood and then accept the emerging adults as nestmates. This habit appears to have been strengthened into obligatory interspecific raiding in the case of *L. duloticus* (Wilson, 1975b; Stuart and Alloway, 1982).

Insect castes and kin selection. The most advanced social insects—bees, wasps, ants, and termites—are characterized by the presence of a sterile worker caste. How could such a system evolve if the workers leave no offspring? Here Darwin encountered the "one special difficulty, which at first appeared insuperable, and actually fatal to my whole theory" (*Origin,* p. 236). Once again, however, he squirmed free and, in so doing, not only saved the theory of natural selection, but added a rich new dimension to evolutionary theory. Darwin found the needed clue in the selective breeding of domestic plants and animals:

This difficulty, though appearing insuperable, is lessened, or, as I believe, disappears, when it is remembered that selection may be applied to the family, as well as to the individual, and may thus gain the desired end. Thus, a well-flavoured vegetable is cooked, and the individual is destroyed; but the horticulturist sows seeds of the same stock, and confidently expects to get nearly the same variety; breeders of cattle wish the flesh and fat to be well marbled together; the animal has been slaughtered, but the breeder goes with confidence to the same family.

Darwin here has anticipated the modern principle of kin selection leading to altruism. In some way, the individual sacrifices itself—the worker ant becomes a neuter caste or the ox is slaughtered—and the act of sacrifice is in a form that favors relatives. Hence the hereditary material that made the sacrificial act probable is multiplied disproportionately, and the trait spreads through the population.

With the help of Frederick Smith, the British Museum entomologist who was an authority on ants (and a poor one, I might add), Darwin considered the possible evolutionary steps that might have led to the extreme caste systems found in *Anomma* driver ants, *Zacryptocerus* tree ants, and *Myrmecocystus* honeypot ants. He noted that in most species a more primitive form of variation exists among the workers of the same colony, especially in size and body shape. This differentiation of sterile offspring can be viewed as a property of the fertile queen and male; they have the inherited capacity to make workers of different kinds. Through the collateral form of selection just described, this capacity was expanded until forms were produced that are radically different in anatomy and behavior from the parents. Darwin figuratively took a deep breath, admitted his own "overweening confidence in the principle of natural selection," and concluded:

With these facts before me, I believe that natural selection, by acting on the fertile parents, could form a species which should regularly produce neuters, either all of large size with one form of jaw, or all of small size with jaws having a widely different structure; or lastly, and this is the climax of our difficulty, one set of workers of one size and structure, and simultaneously another set of workers of different size and structure. . . .

Later research on caste determination and evolution (reviewed by Oster and Wilson, 1978; Brian, 1979) has borne out Darwin's essential conclusions. His reasoning laid the groundwork for modern studies in kin selection that have illuminated not only the evolution of the social insects, but also altruism and other forms of social behavior in all kinds of animals.

Interpopulational selection. The basic arguments on the evolution of insect caste systems can be called a form of group selection, in the sense that one cluster of individuals, the colony, is pitted against another. But in another sense more directly relevant to evolutionary theory, the unit of selection remains the individual—in this case, the mated queen of the colony. The infertile worker can be regarded as an extension of her own personal reproductive effort, as Darwin observed. The workers are genetically as different from her as offspring are from their parents in nonsocial organisms, but they nevertheless share half their genes due to common descent (the other half come from the father, who incidentally in the termites remains in the nest as the "king"). Among the genes are those that predispose some of the offspring, under appropriate nutritional and other environmental conditions, to develop into workers. Their sacrifice is then paid off by the increased reproductive rate of the queen, the greater number of new queens and colonies produced by their own colony, and hence an increase in the frequency of their own genes in the population of colonies at large. The evolution of insect castes can be more properly labeled kin selection rather than selection entailing entire populations; in social insects, the true Darwinian population is not the membership of a given colony, but rather the entire population of colonies—which are competing with each other in the race to produce new colonies. Among the modern developments in the theory of kin selection are the seminal articles by Hamilton (1964, 1972), who showed the close correspondence of the results expected from theory to the actual facts of insect social organization.

It is also possible to have a competition among entire populations of organisms, with some declining and facing extinction while others expand and fill the newly vacated space. If mutations arising within a particular population enhance the fitness of both carrier individuals and others around it, the entire group will expand, and the gene will be multiplied rapidly. This is particularly likely to be the case in species that show social behavior and therefore communicate the beneficial information and behavior of the mutants more efficiently. Such interpopulational selection might be especially favorable for the evolution of intelligence and social cooperation. It can also promote altruism, because even if the mutant individuals themselves are not favored, they can help others in the population and enhance the increase in the overall population. And if the mutant genes are shared by relatives, the new trait might be spread throughout the ensemble of populations as a whole, eventually becoming a species-wide trait. This mixture of interpopulational selection (or group selection, as it is sometimes called) *and* kin selection was clearly visualized as a theoretical possibility by Darwin, who speculated in *The Descent of Man* as follows:

Now, if some one man in a tribe, more sagacious than the others, invented a new snare or weapon, or other means of attack or defense, the plainest self-interest, without the assistance of much reasoning power, would prompt the other members to imitate him; and all would thus profit. The habitual practice of each new art must likewise in some slight degree strengthen the intellect. If the invention were an important one, the tribe would increase in number, spread, and supplant other tribes. In a tribe thus rendered more numerous there would always be a rather greater chance of the birth of other superior and inventive members. If such men left children to inherit their mental superiority, the chance of the birth of still more ingenious members would be somewhat better, and in a very small tribe decidely better. Even if they left no children, the tribe would still include their blood-relations, and it has been ascertained by agriculturists that by preserving and breeding from the family of an animal, which when slaughtered was found to be valuable, the desired character has been obtained.

The process of interpopulational selection has proved extraordinarily difficult to evaluate theoretically, because of the technical problems of computing the effects of natural selection when it operates on two levels at once. It has been even less tractable to realistic experimental analysis. At the present time, ecologists and sociobiologists generally consider it to be at most a minority phenomenon, with selection operating primarily or exclusively at the individual level in most conceivable cases, and kin selection taking a significant auxiliary role in social species. Nevertheless, theoretical studies with sufficiently complex models have defined a range of values in population extinction rates, individual-level selection pressure, and other key parameters within which interpopulational selection becomes influential (Levins, 1965; Boorman and Levitt, 1973; Gilpin, 1975; D. S. Wilson, 1980). Furthermore, as stressed by Alexander (1979) and others, human social behavior and population structure does appear to fall close to the prescribed parameter values. Darwin's intuition was essentially sound. However, he may not have been right. A great deal more research will have to be conducted on both animal and human populations before the role of selection above the level of the individual and kin networks can be properly assessed.

Sexual selection. Darwin's contribution to our understanding of sex differences and courtship behavior has proved seminal with reference to both social and nonsocial animals. With modern refinements added, no phenomenon illustrates better the revolutionary change brought to biological thought.

The modern view of this special form of natural selection can be summarized very briefly as follows (for more extensive treatment, see Daly and M. Wilson, 1978; Symons, 1979; O'Donald, 1980). Because females—by definition—contribute more to each fertilization, they are able to participate in fewer procreations. The average woman, for example, launches only about four hundred eggs into her uterus during her lifetime, but every physiologically normal man releases millions of spermatozoans every time he ejaculates. As a result, one male has the capacity to participate in a vastly greater number of fertilizations than a female.

Some important consequences follow from this elementary difference between the sexes. Perhaps the most basic is that males have a good deal more to gain by competing for mates. A Don Juan can theoretically become a father every night. But if he succeeds in achieving many fertilizations, a corresponding number of males must fail to become fathers. It is therefore not surprising to find that in a large percentage of animal species, and in many human societies as well, males compete aggressively with each other for territory, status, and, above all, access to females. A strong selection pressure exists to create, in Darwin's expression, "the power to charm the ladies" and "the power to conquer other males in battle." This sexual selection is a unique process that Darwin first recognized in the *Origin* and proceeded to examine at length in *The Descent of Man.*

Darwin correctly distinguished sexual selection as a principal category apart from the remainder of the evolutionary process. He perceived that whereas success in ordinary natural selection depends heavily on the moment-by-moment enhancement of survival, males engaged in sexual selection tend to throw caution to the winds, risking their lives openly in conspicuous displays and heedless fighting. Many, like the honeybee drone, purchase a successful mating literally at the cost of their lives. Some of the most beautiful sights and sounds of nature (that is, beautiful to the human senses) consist of the bright colors, songs, and dances of male birds, butterflies, frogs, and other kinds of animals that communicate by audiovisual means. If we had a highly developed sense of smell, we would have an equal appreciation of the complex medleys of pheromones that fill the air.

This great evolutionary flourish has arisen from a form of competition that is basically different from the struggle for ordinary resources. We now understand that conventional competitive techniques evolve as part of density-dependent population controls (see, for example, Wilson, 1975a). Among most species of plants and animals, population numbers are regulated by density-dependent effects in the following manner: as density increases, some factor progressively lowers the average birth rate, raises the average death rate, or accomplishes both—until, finally, the birth and death rates are equal and population growth halts. Examples of such density-dependent competition include predators (which grow in numbers and efficiency), disease (spreading more and more effectively), emigration, and, not least, competition among the members of the species for resources (Ricklefs, 1980; May, 1981). If some factor, such as predation or disease, regularly brings population growth to zero, ordinary competition behavior may never evolve. In fact, some insect species are known in which competition seems rarely, if ever, to occur. And this is precisely the aspect in which sexual selection is different. It comprises a form of competition that does not directly involve density-dependent controls. Sexual selection can be highly developed in species that otherwise never compete. The forms of behavior that it entails are often radically different.

To generalize the matter very simply, males of species with intense sexual selection are typically reckless, boastful, and very intolerant of being cheated. With reference to the human case, we may note that adultery is the leading cause of murder in more primitively organized human societies. In a few species—for example, the *dendrobatid* ("poison arrow" frogs of Central and South America) and various jacanas, tinamous, and phalaropes among the birds—the females compete for males, largely because the males have assumed an important role in care of the young. In conformity with sexual selection theory, they are the bold competitors and advertisers. In most species of higher animals, including primates, females still participate in sexual selection, but with different goals and strategies (Hrdy, 1981). They can be inseminated in a given reproductive season by one male, and they usually have the greater burden of looking after the young. Therefore, it is to their advantage to be discriminating: flirtatious to attract many suitors, but at the same time, coy, reticent, and perceptive in order to mate with the best of males. The "best," in this case, usually means the most competent in dealing with other males. Among those species in which males help to rear the young, it further means the mate most likely to devote himself to nurture. In social groups, females also engage in power relationships to gain advantages for themselves and their offspring and other close kin.

Animal communication. In *The Expression of the Emotions in Man and Animals* (1872), Darwin put into place a substantial part of the foundation of ethology and sociobiology by showing the way toward the comparative studies of instinct (Marler, 1959; Thorpe, 1979). In the course of this work, he formulated the first principles of the evolution of communication and established the plausibility of the genetic control of behavioral traits, which can be employed with the same logic as that applied to anatomical and physiological traits in the reconstruction of evolution. He saw the expression of human emotions, especially through the species-wide facial expressions, as being especially favorable for future research. This proposal has since borne fruit (see, for example, Ekman, 1973). Konrad Lorenz (1965), one of the founders of modern ethology, could thus state with conviction that the field "has a right to claim Charles Darwin as its patron saint. It is more immediately dependent on the selectionistic approach than any other biological science I could name, and it has done its fair share in verifying Darwin's theories. Furthermore, in his book, *The Expression of the Emotions in Man and Animals,* Charles Darwin has foreseen in a truly visionary manner the main problems which confront ethologists to this day and has mapped out a strategy of research which they still use."

Adventures Remaining

There are two major questions of sociobiology to which Darwin was not in a position to contribute in any significant degree. The first is the intensity of the optimization process in natural selection, and the second is the nature of the interaction of natural selection with cultural evolution in the formation of human societies. The pursuit of these problems awaited new information and techniques that became available in the twentieth century.

Optimization. We all know that natural selection has shaped the structure of an ant colony, but how well does the colony function relative to what *might* be evolved? Or, to ask a more tractable form of the question, how closely adapted is the colony to the local environment? How well fitted is it to the imperatives and opportunities of the species niche? The solution does not lie in the identification of global optima. One can imagine ants with large brains, wings that fold into grooves, and iron-hard mandibles. But such advances would require major reorganizations of the formicide genotype that lay beyond its reach throughout the 100 million years of microevolution and speciation that actually occurred. The more realistic and interesting question is the degree to which microevolution has fitted particular species to the niches in which they find themselves.

Optimization studies employing both mathematical models and experimentation have gained prominence during the past ten years in ethology, behavioral ecology, and sociobiology (Oster and Wilson, 1978; Krebs and Davies, 1981; McFarland and Houston, 1981). The procedure generally consists in the following steps:

1. The investigator selects a species for its interesting natural history and apparent tractability to experimentation.

2. The investigator studies its behavior and ecology and proposes hypotheses concerning the adaptiveness of particular behavioral acts, such as foraging, orientation, and communication.

3. Then the investigator lists multiple competing hypotheses concerning the principal selection pressures that molded the behavioral act of interest. These pressures define the *criteria* by which optimization in microevolution can be assessed. Examples of criteria include number of mates acquired, net energetic yield during foraging, and probability of death by predation. Suppose that a species forages only at a certain hour near dawn. The principal criterion may well be either predator avoidance, which is most easily accomplished at that time, or accessibility of food, or both.

4. The investigator devises measurements and experiments to determine which of the imagined criteria, if any, are satisfied and how close to the conceivable optimum the species has evolved.

The final step of this sequence, in which the approach to the conceivable optimum is assessed, is the most difficult to achieve. In ideal circumstances, the experience should be able to create mutants of the species, which deviate in small increments away from the normal behavior, and then proceed to compare their performance. For example, if a certain animal that forages at 0300–0500 hours can be made to forage at

0100–0300 or 0500–0700 hours, we ask: will its net energetic yield (or avoidance of predators, or whatever) increase or decrease—and by how much?

At first, such an idealized experimental program might seem impossible to achieve. It is difficult enough to alter the behavior of animals in such a directed manner without changing other aspects of their behavior or the environment itself. However, by selecting the appropriate species and techniques, the procedure can be followed. In a recent study of foraging in the leafcutter ant *Atta sexdens* (Wilson, E. O., 1980), for example, I took advantage of the fact that the ant colony is a superorganism. It is possible to tear apart a superorganism and put it back together again in a way that is impossible with ordinary organisms. The queen or minor worker population can be removed, the effect of their absence studied, and then the colony reconstituted for further control measurements. In contrast, the ovaries or brain of a single ant cannot be ablated and restored with anything approaching equivalent ease.

I noted the two additional facts of importance in this particular case: most leaf cutting and retrieval is conducted by *Atta sexdens* workers with head widths of about 2.2 mm (within a total colony size range of 0.6 to 5.5 mm), and workers of this size perform few other tasks. In other words, 2.2 mm workers are highly specialized for that particular function. But is this the *optimum* size group to perform the task? Has the *Atta sexdens* caste system evolved so as to maximize foraging efficiency? In accordance with the procedures outlined earlier, I listed a series of conceivable criteria: speed in foraging, defense against predators, and net energetic yield. I then created pseudomutants of the *Atta* colony in the following way. As the foraging force emerged each day from a laboratory nest to gather fresh vegetation, I removed all but one size class and then measured its performance. On one day, the foraging group consisted exclusively of workers with 1.6 mm head widths; the next day, they were all 3.0 mm; on the next day, all were 2.2 mm;

and so on for numerous replications of each size group. Measurements were taken of their initiative and efficiency during cutting, dry weight (to ascertain construction costs), and oxygen consumption (a measure of maintenance costs). At the end of each trial, the working force and the colony as a whole were restored to their original constitution. The procedure is roughly the equivalent of measuring the efficiency of hands of various forms in the use of a tool: one day, a sixth finger is added (and then painlessly removed at the end of the experiment); the next day, all the fingers are (painlessly) trimmed to the first joint and restored afterward; and so on through many "pseudomutant" forms to determine their effectiveness in handling the tool. It would be extremely difficult to do just that with a real hand or any other organ, but its equivalent is easily managed with an insect colony.

The principal result of the *Atta* study was the demonstration that the most energetically efficient size group is indeed that with a modal head width of 2.2 mm. The colony is evidently at an optimum with respect to the net energetic yield during foraging, apparently without any significant compromise to predator avoidance or any other criterion that was imagined. I then asked whether further microevolution could be accomplished by *Atta sexdens* in a way that shifts the optimum to another size group, raising the net energetic yield even more. Employing a simple mathematical model, I altered a key behavioral trait by equalizing the initiative of all the size groups. If such a microevolutionary change were to occur in reality, the energetically most efficient caste would be at 2.6–2.8 mm, or about 10 percent greater than the size of the actual caste employed. Why the *Atta* have not shifted to this somewhat higher point during their evolution I do not know, but the fit is still remarkably close. I believe that the results of the experiment represent one of the first demonstrations that a species is not only genetically adapted, but is actually perched near the top of a local adaptive peak. In other words, it is not only

at an optimum, but also—and the distinction is important—
it has been optimized.

Gene-culture coevolution. Until very recently, there has
been no way to place human cognition and culture within the
framework of evolutionary biology. Many writers prefer to
think that such an accommodation is impossible, or irrelevant,
and that as a consequence, the social sciences must be perma-
nently independent from biology. But this view is no longer
defensible. Of course, we must acknowledge that variation in
human social behavior is relatively enormous. It is also subject
to rapid change in response to cultural innovation and imita-
tion. Cultural evolution is often characterized as Lamarckian
in nature (meaning that it is dependent on the transmission of
acquired characters and occurs relatively quickly), while genetic evolution is Darwinian (in other words, it is dependent
on changes in gene frequencies across generations and takes
place slowly). But exactly how are the two processes coupled?

The key to the problem lies in shifting emphasis from the
final results of the two processes—that is, the genome on one
side and culture on the other—and concentrating on the intervening development. The reason why such an analysis has
not proceeded more vigorously in the past is that evolutionary
biologists have virtually ignored developmental psychology,
which is now a vast field in its own right, while psychologists
for their part have not appreciated the great potential of evolutionary analysis.

Recently Charles J. Lumsden and I proposed a theory of
"gene-culture coevolution" to characterize the linkage between genetic and cultural change (Lumsden and Wilson,
1981, 1983). The main conception can be characterized as
follows. First, human genes affect the way the mind is formed
—which stimuli we perceive, how information is processed,
the kind of memories most easily stored and recalled, the
emotions they are most likely to evoke, and so on. These
effects, which have been well documented in psychological

research, are called epigenetic rules. The rules are rooted in the particularities of human biology, and they affect the way culture is formed. For example, outbreeding is much more likely to occur than brother-sister incest because of the apparently innate rule that individuals raised closely together during the first six years of life are inhibited from full sexual intercourse at maturity. Certain color vocabularies are more likely to be adopted than others because of another rule: the retinal color cones and certain interneurons of the lateral geniculate nuclei encode light into four basic colors, even when the wavelengths of light falling on the eye varies in a continuous manner. The Dani of New Guinea have one of the poorest color vocabularies in the world—in fact, it consists of only two terms, one for bright and one for dark. Eleanor Rosch (1973) took advantage of this fact to conduct an experiment in learning propensity. She gave one group of volunteers a new color vocabulary to learn in which the terms were centered on the four basic colors. Another group received a vocabulary centered on the wavelengths at the margins of the basic colors. Individuals in the first, "natural" group learned the words twice as quickly and retained them longer. When given a choice between the two terminologies, Dani men preferred the natural vocabulary. Both of these cases, incest avoidance and the development of color vocabularies, illustrate nicely how biological constraints in cognition, based on specific genes, can influence the formation of culture. Moreover, epigenetic rules have been demonstrated in virtually every category of cognition and behavior investigated by psychologists in such a way as to distinguish choices among stimuli.

In order to visualize the essential steps of gene-culture co-evolution, consider the particular case of the avoidance of brother-sister incest. Because this epigenetic rule occurs across cultures and is strong enough to defeat countervailing social pressures, it can reasonably be supposed to have a genetic basis. Furthermore, those who follow the rule benefit in natural selection. Incest results in higher rates of homozygosity, the more frequent expression of lethal or subvital recessive genes, and hence a greater incidence of hereditary disease and early death among the offspring.

The epigenetic rule thus directs the developing mind to avoid brother-sister incest. The summed preferences of members of the society lead to particular cultural patterns, including reinforcing taboos and laws, that prohibit incest. However, because the preference is not absolute, a few members in many societies still prefer and may even practice brother-sister incest. The result is some variation among cultures in the percentage of its members who practice incest. The pattern of the variation—the number and position of the modes and the amount of variation—can be predicted from a knowledge of the amount of bias in the preference for one cultural choice (such as incest) versus another (outbreeding) and the degree to which the expressed preference of the remainder of the group affects the magnitude of the individual bias. It is important to note that cultural diversity *per se* is evidence neither for nor against biological effects. Rather, what matters is the pattern of cultural diversity and its correspondence to the observed epigenetic rules of individual cognitive development.

Thus the genes affect the formation of mind and culture through the epigenetic rules. The reverse process completes the coevolutionary circuit. The epigenetic rules are shaped by genetic evolution, and especially natural selection, over many generations. In the example of brother-sister incest, individuals who conform to the aversion (and the reinforcing taboos and laws) leave more offspring. As a result, genes underwriting the avoidance of incest remain at a high level in the population. Consequently, the predisposition is sustained as one of the epigenetic rules. In general, those rules leading to higher rates of survival and reproduction tend to increase in the population. Thus the epigenetic rules of the mind build up during evolution. Lumsden and I have created pilot models from this basic theory that predict the direction and rate of change in gene frequencies during episodes of gene-culture coevolution.

If evolutionary theory can be successfully extended to embrace key features of cognition and ethnography, the remarkable wave of investigation that Darwin inaugurated can be fairly said to have reached a new level, one that insures the ultimate conjunction of the biological and social sciences.

REFERENCES

Alexander, R. D. 1979. *Darwinism and human affairs.* Seattle: University of Washington Press.

Boorman, S. A., and Levitt, P. R. 1973. Group selection on the boundary of a stable population. *Proceedings of the National Academy of Sciences, U.S.A.* 69:2711–13.

Brian, M. V. 1979. Caste differentiation and division of labor. In *Social insects,* vol. 1, Ed. H. R. Hermann, pp. 121–22. New York: Academic Press.

Buschinger, A. 1981. Biological and systematic relationships of social parasitic Leptothoracini from Europe and North America. In *Biosystematics of social insects,* eds. P. E. Howse and J. L. Clemént, pp. 211–22. New York: Academic Press.

Daly, M., and Wilson, M. 1978. *Sex, evolution, and behavior: adaptations for reproduction.* North Scituate, Mass.: Duxbury Press.

Darwin, C. R. 1859. *On the origin of species.* London: John Murray.

Darwin, C. R. 1871. *The descent of man, and selection in relation to sex.* 2 vols. New York: Appleton.

Darwin, C. R. 1872. *The expression of the emotions in man and animals.* New York: Appleton.

Ekman, P. 1973. Cross-cultural studies of facial expression. In *Darwin and facial expression: a century of research in review,* ed. P. Ekman, pp. 169–222. New York: Academic Press.

Gilpin, M. E. 1975. *Group selection in predator-prey communities.* Princeton, N.J.: Princeton University Press.

Hamilton, W. D. 1964. The genetical evolution of social behavior, I, II. *Jo. Theoretical Biology* 7:1–52.

Hamilton, W. D. 1972. Altruism and related phenomena, mainly in social insects. *Ann. Rev. Ecology and Systematics* 3:193–232.

Hrdy, S. B. 1981. *The woman that never evolved.* Cambridge, Mass.: Harvard University Press.

Huber, P. 1810. *Recherches sur les moeurs des fourmis indigènes.* Paris: J. J. Paschoud.

Krebs, J. R., and Davies, N. B. 1981. *An introduction to behavioral ecology.* Boston: Blackwell.

Levins, R. 1965. *Evolution in a changing environment: some theoretical explorations.* Princeton, N.J.: Princeton University Press.

Lindauer, M. 1971. *Communication among social bees.* Cambridge, Mass.: Harvard University Press.

Lorenz, K. 1965. Preface to *The expression of the emotions in man and animals,* by C. R. Darwin, pp. ix–xiii. Chicago: University of Chicago Press (Phoenix Books).

Lumsden, C. J., and Wilson, E. O. 1981. *Genes, mind, and culture.* Cambridge, Mass.: Harvard University Press.

Lumsden, C. J., and Wilson, E. O., 1983 (in press). *The fourth step.* Cambridge, Mass.: Harvard University Press.

Marler, P. R. 1959. Developments in the study of animal communication. In *Darwin's Biological Work,* Ed. P. R. Bell. Cambridge, England: Cambridge University Press.

May, R. M. 1981. Models for simple populations. In *Theoretical ecology: principles and applications,* ed. R. M. May, pp. 5–29. 2d ed. Boston: Blackwell.

Mayr, E. 1964. Introduction to *On the origin of species,* pp. vii–xxvii. 1st ed. facsimile. Cambridge, Mass.: Harvard University Press.

McFarland, D., and Houston, A. 1981. *Quantitative ethology: the state space approach.* Boston: Pitman.

Michener, C. D. 1974. *The social behavior of the bees: a comparative study.* Cambridge, Mass.: Harvard University Press (Belknap Press).

O'Donald, P. 1980. *Genetic models of sexual selection.* Cambridge, England: Cambridge University Press.

Oster, G. F., and Wilson, E. O. 1978. *Caste and ecology in the social insects.* Princeton, N.J.: Princeton University Press.

Ricklefs, R. E. 1980. *Ecology.* 2d ed. Sudbury-on-Thames, England: Thomas Nelson and Sons.

Rosch, E. 1973. Natural categories. *Cognitive Psychology* 4:328–50.

Stuart, R. J., and Alloway, T. M. 1982. Territoriality and the origin of slave raiding in leptothoracine ants. *Science* 215:1262–63.

Symons, D. 1979. *The evolution of human sexuality.* New York: Oxford University Press.

Thorpe, W. H. 1979. *The origins and rise of ethology: the science of the natural behavior of animals.* London: Heinemann Educational Books.

Wilson, D. S. 1980. *The natural selection of populations and communities.* Menlo Park, Calif.: Benjamin/Cummings.

Wilson, E. O. 1971. *The insect societies.* Cambridge, Mass.: Harvard University Press (Belknap Press).

Wilson, E. O. 1975a. *Sociobiology: the new synthesis.* Cambridge, Mass.: Harvard University Press (Belknap Press).

Wilson, E. O. 1975b. *Leptothorax duloticus* and the beginnings of slavery in ants. *Evolution* 29:108–119.

Wilson, E. O. 1980. Caste and division of labor in leaf-cutter ants (Hymenoptera: Formicidae: *Atta*). II. The ergonomic optimization of leaf cutting. *Behavioral Ecology and Sociobiology* 7(2):157–65.

Darwin's Legacy: Emanation, Evolution, and Development

JAROSLAV PELIKAN

This conference on "Darwin's Legacy" is itself a part of the legacy of Darwin, for all of us, not only those of us like myself who are by profession scholars in intellectual history, regard it now altogether natural to treat scientific theories, philosophical systems, political ideas, theological doctrines, and other sets of thoughts as the products of an evolutionary process. For example, the distinguished British medievalist and Benedictine monk, my friend and colleague, Dom David Knowles, Regius Professor of Modern History in the University of Cambridge, could entitle his most widely circulated book *The Evolution of Medieval Thought*. It is, then, an acknowledgment of that legacy to examine what might be called "the evolution of evolution," and to do so on the basis of this intriguing historical coincidence.

In his introduction to *The Origin of Species by Means of Natural Selection*, Charles Darwin tells us that he had enlarged his earlier "short notes" about the subject "into a sketch of the conclusions, which then seemed to me probable," and that he had done so in 1844. It was in that same year, on July 14, 1844, that John Henry Newman set down "the general view to which I came," as stated in a letter of that date:

Granting that the Roman [Catholic] (special) doctrines [those which separate Roman Catholicism from other Christian traditions] are not found drawn out in the early Church, yet I think there is sufficient trace of them in it, to recommend and prove them, on the hypothesis of the Church having a divine guidance, though not sufficient to prove them by itself. . . . The analogy of the Old Testament, and also of the New, leads to the acknowledgement of doctrinal development.

Describing his own development in 1844, Newman adds in his autobiography, *Apologia pro Vita Sua,* of 1864: "And thus I was led on to a further consideration. I saw that the principle of development not only accounted for certain facts, [in the issue with which he was dealing] but was in itself a remarkable philosophical phenomenon." Each in its own way, then, Darwin's "sketch" of 1844 and Newman's "general view" of this remarkable philosophical phenomenon of 1844, have contributed (have not by themselves caused) to a shift in our perspective on reality, from Being to Becoming, from timeless reality to temporal process, from eternal stasis to historical evolution and development.

The earliest evidences for "the evolution of evolution" in the fossil record of the English language (otherwise known as the Oxford English dictionary) occur in the writings of the seventeenth-century Cambridge Platonists, Henry More and Ralph Cudworth. More spoke in a poem of 1647, which is probably the first time the word *Evolution* is used as an English word, about the "evolution of outward forms spread in the world's vast spright," and in his *Divine Dialogues* of 1667, he wrote, "the whole evolution . . . of ages, from everlasting to everlasting, is . . . represented to God at once." Ralph Cudworth, More's slightly younger contemporary (but probably also his teacher), similarly declared in his massive opus, *The True Intellectual System of the Universe,* written over a long period of time, published only in 1677: "The periods of divine Providence, here in this world, are commonly longer, and the evolution thereof slower." From these passages, it is evident that in the earliest stages of its own evolution as an English word, *evolution* was closely related to, and seems sometimes to have been virtually identical with, the Neoplatonic concept of emanation. Significantly, Henry More is also one of the earliest witnesses for the use of *emanation* as an English word: "Man's soul's not by creation. . . . Wherefore let it be by emanation," he said.

The concept of emanation-as-evolution in the thought of the Cambridge Platonists was based on their notion of "plastic nature." There was, according to Cudworth, a fundamental difference between the operations of nature and those of what he calls "human art." For while human ingenuity and skill, in order to work on something, must operate "from without and at a distance," nature was itself "an inward principle" in matter, which, by "insinuating itself immediately [without a medium] into the things themselves, . . . does its work easily, cleverly, and silently." It was, he quoted from Aristotle's *Physics,* as if "the ship-building art were in the wood" rather than in the carpenter. That was how "plastic nature" caused change to happen, through the actualization of a potential that was already somehow present within the matter rather than through the imposition upon it of form and direction by some external agent. And if you hear echoes of Plato's *Timaes* in this, you are right, of course. Cudworth further defined this "plastic nature" by equating it with what Plotinus and others had called "seminal reason-forms" (the Greek is λόγοι σπερματικοί, "logoi spermatikoi"), an extremely important concept in Neoplatonic Jewish and Christian thought, and he quoted the *Enneads* of Plotinus to prove that plastic nature was not, on the other hand, to be equated with the "absolute divine intellect" or with the Creator God of Christian doctrine, but was in fact "something which depends" on God. Therefore, the idea of "plastic nature," he said, had been "mistaken, perverted, and abused by those theists who would make it to be the only God Almighty or first principle of all things." It was rather, in Platonic terms, the form of the forms of which particular empirical entities are then the manifestation. And God creates the form of forms from which then the forms for particulars proceed, from which then, in turn, the particulars themselves come. An old idea that attempts to blend Neoplatonic and biblical world-views.

Although not to be identified with God, then, "plastic nature" did "contain no small part of divine providence in it." Henry More, in the preface to his treatise of 1659, *The Immortality of the Soul,* spoke of "the vicarious power of God upon the matter," a term that E. A. Burtt has aptly paraphrased as "the immediate plastic agent of God through which God's will is fulfilled in the material world." That is plastic nature. More's contemporary and colleague, John Smith, formulated the doctrine of creation in his *Discourses* of 1660. "God," he insisted, "hath never thrown the world from himself, but runs through all created essence." Within himself, therefore, God contained "the archetypical ideas of all things," from which in turn there came the "several prints of beauty and excellency all the world over." The universe and all particular creatures were mirrors of God, "wherein he might reflect his own glory." Smith maintained that "a soul that is truly θεοειδης, 'godlike,' a mind that is enlightened from the same fountain . . . cannot but everywhere behold itself in the midst of that glorious, unbounded Being who is indivisibly everywhere." Because "every created excellency is a beam descending from the Father of lights" (James 1:17), it followed that "we should love all things in God and God in all things, because he is all in all, the beginning and the original of being, the perfect idea of their goodness and the end of their motion."

In his posthumously published *Treatise Concerning Eternal and Immutable Morality* (1731), Cudworth presented his own version of what Smith had called "a soul that is truly . . . 'godlike,' " by describing "all particular created intellects" as "but derivative participations" in the mind of God the Creator. As derivative participation, the human mind was able to perceive the truth of the divine mind. This it did through both revelation and reason; for, in one of the *Aphorisms* of Benjamin Whichcote, who was the teacher of most of the Cambridge Platonists, "God hath set up two lights to enlighten us in our way: the light of reason, which is the light of his creation, and the light of Scripture, which is after-revelation from him. Let us make use of these two lights and let us suffer neither of them to be put out." They weren't all listening to that. "If you would be religious," he said in a later aphorism, "the perfection of the happiness of human nature consists in the right use of our rational faculties, in the vigorous and intense exercise of them about their proper and proportionable object, which is God." As my Australian colleague Professor David Dockrill has observed, "for Whichcote, any doctrine which offends the principles of right reason . . . is a doctrine which is to be rejected on the ground that it is inconsistent with known truth." Whichcote and his pupils took it for granted that there could not be a fundamental contradiction between the "after-revelation" contained in Scripture, if properly understood, and these principles of right reason. Both the nature of reality and the definition of truth must conform to that essential harmony.

Nevertheless, both the reality and the truth about the reality, both the creation and the revelation, while in one sense given once and for all, were also continuing through time and history. To borrow (and adapt) a statement from Arthur Lovejoy to some medieval writers whom he doesn't specify, "It was becoming increasingly evident—as it had, indeed, been that something had to be done to fit the postulate . . . with the fact that the concrete world *is* temporal. The assumed necessity was an *eternal* necessity; but its execution, so to say, manifestly was *not* eternal." The various pre-Darwinian theories of evolution summarized by Lovejoy, such as those of Leibniz, Robinet, and others, were all efforts to achieve what Lovejoy calls, in reference to Immanuel Kant, a "temporalized version" of an eternal principle. What Lovejoy neglects to point out (unless those are the medieval writers he is talking about) is that in the history of Christian Platonism and, for that matter, of Jewish Platonism as well, there had long been a tension between an essentially atemporal doctrine of evolution-as-emanation, which was unrelated to temporal process, and the literary form of the biblical account of creation in six discreet days. Both Philo of Alexandria, on the Jewish side, and Augustine of Hippo, on the Christian side, for example, had sought to resolve the problem by an exegesis of the Book of Genesis in which the six days were taken to be symbolic for an instantaneous act of divine creation, in which, as Gilson says, "God creates everything simultaneously." This had been one of the Augustinian ideas that came under the gentle but firm criticism of Thomas Aquinas, who cited Augustine's "opinion that all the days that are called seven are one day represented in a sevenfold aspect," but who came out instead in support of the sequential creation in which, moreover, "one day is made up of twenty-four hours." I should perhaps point out, in the light of subsequent history, that the most influential thinker in the history of the Christian church since the first century, Augustine of Hippo, thus refused to read the Genesis account of creation literally and that when he was criticized for it by one of the other most influential thinkers since the first century, St. Thomas, he was criticized but not hereticized. It took the Reformation to change that.

At a previous Darwin centennial, in 1959, at the University of Chicago, I gave some attention to how these several "temporalized versions" of evolution fared when they collided with the doctrine of creation in six days of twenty-four hours each. It is a topic to which I shall have to return elsewhere. I should note in the context of this paper that it was the application of Cardinal Newman's ideas of development and progressive revelation to the doctrine of creation that led in this century to a way out of the cul-de-sac. And let me raise an historical question to which I really don't have an answer, but which I find intriguing. To paraphrase Patrick Henry, Catholicism had its Galileo, and Protestantism had its Darwin, and each had that as its particular bête noire—and why should it have been that the heliocentric theory of the universe was more troubling in Catholic than in Protestant thought, and that evolution was more troubling in Protestant than in Catholic thought? This is an issue that's really much more subtle than I can handle in a throwaway obiter dictum, but it's worth thinking about. And it's still the case, incidentally. My interest here lies in another aspect of the history. For it was not only the doctrine of emanation-as-evolution, as developed by the Cambridge Platonists, that was being "temporalized" in the nineteenth century through Darwin and others, but it was also their doctrine of reason-revelation. Both of these were changed from a point to a line. If one could presuppose Greek, which one can't, they were changed from an aorist to an imperfect. In the doctrine of revelation, moreover, this "temporalizing" was calling attention not only to the relation between the history of the Hebrew Bible and the history of the Christian New Testament (as successive stages of a revelation to be called "progressive," with a little bit more revealed each time), but now also to the relation between *all* of biblical revelation, whether Old Testament or New, and the successive ages of history since the death of the last apostle. For this, too, must be seen as, in some sense, "progressive." It was the historic achievement of John Henry Newman to have made this latter relation the focus of his attention in a book called *An Essay on the Development of Christian Doctrine,* published in 1845. He wrote it as an Anglican, and while it was in the presses, he became a Roman Catholic—a prime example of taking your scholarship far too seriously.

Like his contemporary, Robert William Dale, who wrote that "the Christian faith may be spoken of as, in some sense, the development of Judaism," Newman said that "the Gospel is the development of the Law," since "the prophetic revelation is . . . a process of development," rather than a series of disclosures, not on the installment plan, in which "first one truth is told, and then another." Rather, it develops, and "the event which is the development is also the interpretation of the prediction." Newman employed that word *development* in an innovative and, I think, unique fashion (at least, I don't know predecessors for it), both for the process and for the result of the postbiblical history of Christian doctrine.

In one of his most characteristic and revealing statements about development, Newman identified as "the simplist, the most natural, and the most persuasive" theory of the history of Christian doctrine "the notion of development under infallible authority." Obviously, the "infallible authority" part of that definition was of the utmost consequence to him, both in his interpretation of the notion of development and in the personal consequences that in 1845 he felt obliged to draw from that notion, when he finally became a Roman Catholic. In this lecture, I am not paying attention to Newman's doctrine of authority, except incidentally; nor shall I repeat here what I have written elsewhere on the implication of Newman's idea of development for the general methodology of the history of ideas. Rather, I want to relate this idea to the ideas of emanation and evolution as I have been summarizing them, and then to draw out some of the similarities and some of the differences between Newman and Darwin in their "temporalized versions" of what had been the chiefly metaphysical doctrines of creation and of revelation.

As in the biological evolution of species, so in the development of ideas and doctrines, there had been a subtle interaction between the internal grounds and the external causes of change: in Newman's summary, "the decision has been left to time, to the slow process of thought, to the influence of mind upon mind, the issues of controversy, and the growth of opinion." It was obvious from history that the external factors had often been decisive. For "no doctrine is defined until it is violated." One of Newman's colleagues, a man named Ward, did not believe that; he wanted all doctrines defined immediately, and he is the origin of Lewis Carroll's character who could believe several impossible things before breakfast. He said he'd like to have an infallible doctrine with his morning egg each day. Presumably an infinite supply of both eggs and infallible dogmas was involved. So heresies, Newman observed, "determine in what way the current is setting, and the rate at which the current flows." For example, there is the doctrine of original sin, a Western doctrine, not an Eastern Christian doctrine, for which Augustine had been embarrassed to find so little support in the three centuries preceding him, not only in the Greek East, but even in the Latin West. That doctrine had, Newman said, been "held back for a time by circumstance, yet in the event [it had forced] its way into its normal shape, and [was] at length authoritatively fixed." Indeed, it would be easy to conclude from the history of this doctrine and of others that they were, Newman says, "a random combination of various opinions," a collection of "deductions and diversions made at random, according to accidents or the caprice of individuals." Now, as far as the individuals themselves were concerned, such a conclusion did have some validity. For "it is often a matter of accident in what order [developments of doctrine] are carried out in individual minds," Newman said, as when the challenge of heresy or "the influence of mind upon mind" in instruction or in controversy gave prominence now to this doctrine, and now to that one. In the light of such "accidents," Newman was obliged to concede:

When we consider the deep interest of the controversies which Christianity raises, the various characters of mind it has swayed, the range of subjects which it embraces, the many countries it has entered, the deep philosophies it has encountered, the vicissitudes it has undergone, and the length of time through which it has lasted, it requires some assignable explanation, why we should not consider it substantially modified and changed, that is, corrupted, from the first, by the numberless influences to which it has been exposed.

The ultimate such "assignable explanation" for Newman was, of course, "the appointment in that [divine] scheme of an external authority to decide upon [developments], thereby separating them from the mass of mere human speculation, extravagance, corruption, and error, in and out of which they grow." "This is," he specified, "the doctrine of the infallibility of the Church." Remember, this was before 1870, the promulgation of the dogma of the infallibility of the pope by the First Vatican Council. From his own researches as an historian, Newman knew that "history is not a creed or a catechism, it gives [us] lessons rather than rules." Thus even, or especially, for a scholar learned in the history of Christian doctrine, the legitimacy of a particular development was not self-authenticating. History worked, if at all, only a posteriori. It could not "be written," he says, "except in an after-age." There must, therefore, be grounds of development that are present within, rather than without, the Christian organism. Newman borrowed terms from biology, as we shall see he often did, in speaking about tradition and development, to describe the course of Christian doctrine as directed "by the guidance, as it were, endemic tradition." Earlier he asserted that "development" as a "process" is "not an effect of wishing and resolving, or of forced enthusiasm, or of any mechanism of reasoning, or of any mere subtlety of intellect, but [came] of its own innate power of expansion within the mind in its season," with an "active, engrossing, and interpenetrating power." But the clinching argument in favor of the inner vitality from which developments came was that in Christianity "developments cannot but be, and those surely divine, because it is divine."

For all his concentration on development, then, Newman was intent on the preservation of continuity, which in various sections of the essay he characterized as "real," as "undeniable," and as a "guarantee." The church had, he maintained, always been "strong . . . from its continuity." Once again, as in the passage just quoted, his argument in support of this continuity was sometimes empirical, as though it were what a historian would do, while at other times he would state it apodictically as an apriori for which no evidence was needed, so that, he tells us, for example, that the apostles in the first century "would without words know all the truths concerning the high doctrines of theology, which controversialists after them have piously and charitably reduced to formulae." He says elsewhere that the doctrine of the double procession of the Holy Ghost, because it came to be taught in 1274, must, in some sense, have been taught all along. And if the historical evidence for so massive an assertion as that was lacking or had not gone through the formality of coming into being, he felt able to resort to his own special version of the argument from silence. Precisely because of the seemingly "random" quality of the development of various doctrines "according to the emergency of the time," it could be maintained, he said, that "silence at a certain period implies not that [a particular doctrine] was not then held, but that it was not being questioned." But the doctrines for which it was permissible to argue from silence in this fashion were only those that had since become, or had finally become, manifest as authoritative Catholic teaching. The doctrine of justification promulgated by the Council of Trent in the sixteenth century in response to the Reformation, for example, was "in some sense . . . new." And so was Luther's doctrine to which it was a response. Trent was, therefore, an illustration of what Newman, near the end of the *Essay,* called, "addition"—that is, "a change which is in one sense real and perceptible, yet without loss or reversal of what was before, but on the contrary, protective and confirmative of it." It was the "characteristic of heresy" to manifest "novelty and originality," and that was "the difference between originality of mind and the gift and calling of a Doctor of the Church." Paradoxically, then, "corruption" could be seen, on the one hand, as the refusal to move with a doctrine as it evolved and, on the other hand, as a synonym for "change." What Newman was describing and advocating against both of these was, in a formula he borrowed from the fifth-century thinker St. Vincent of Lerins, "profectus fidei non permutation"—the progression of doctrine, not its transformation.

This rather exasperating ambivalence between an empirical and an aprioristic methodology in the "scientific" determination of which doctrine represented a transformation and which represented a progression, which doctrines had developed authentically and which doctrines had developed corruptly, which growths were benign and which growths were malignant (to stay with a metaphor he also liked to use) carried over into Newman's treatment of history itself and into his answer to the question that an historian always has to ask himself, "Couldn't the history have come out some other way?" If Cleopatra's nose had been longer, to use Pascal's observation. He could quote Edward Gibbon of whom Newman calls the "melancholy" admission "the only ecclesiastical English writer who has any claim to be considered an ecclesiastical historian is the infidel, Gibbon." Well, he could quote Gibbon in an incident in Byzantian in Constantinople: "the Greeks would perhaps still be involved in heresy if the Emperor's horse had not fortunately stumbled, the Emperor Theodosius expired, and his orthodox sister succeeded to the throne." This passage from Gibbon illustrated, Newman added, "the character of sovereigns, the rise and fall of statesmen, the fate of battles, and the numberless vicissitudes of this world." But that was political history, and, moreover, it was the *Greek* empire and the *Greek* church. When it came to doctrinal history, to that of the Latin church, however, Newman was not prepared to assign to "the numberless vicissitudes of this world" a similarly decisive role. Even beyond his own strict area of special pleading, he could see, in general, "a certain continuous advance and determinate path which belongs to the history of a doctrine, a policy, or an institution." A fortiori was this true of orthodox Catholic doctrine. Here there were "formal, legitimate, and true developments," which Newman defined as "developments contemplated by its Divine Author." If there were indeed "formal, legitimate, and true" developments, then they must likewise be, he says, "natural and necessary." Apparently, then, it really could not have come out any other way than the way it did. At a different speed, perhaps, in a different order, certainly with different formulae and philosophical structures (Newman didn't particularly care for Aristotle or St. Thomas), but not substantially modified and changed from what had in fact become "modern Catholicism."

The tension between empirical research and authoritarian assertion manifests itself above all in the very issue we are examining here: the relation of "development of doctrine" as Newman saw it to the analogous phenomena in other areas of human thought and endeavor, especially to "evolution" in biology as Darwin saw it. Thus Newman spoke of "the general methods by which the course of things is carried forward," to which Christianity, too, could be expected to conform in its development. And he spoke again of "the general probability ... that doctrine cannot but develop as time proceeds and need arises." Echoing the great work of the profound thinker Bishop Joseph Butler, author of the *Analogy of Religion,* which was published in 1736 and which everybody read in the nineteenth century, he appealed to "the general analogy of the world, physical and moral" and to what he calls "the analogy of nature" in support of his theory of doctrinal development. Also from Butler came the analogy between "the truth of our religion" and "the truth of common matters." There was, moreover, "a great law which is seen in developments generally," of which Newman urged: "We must be content to follow the law of our being (which is temporal change) in religious matters as well as in secular." Relying once again on the principle of analogy that he said he had learned from Butler (though not only from Butler, but also from the church fathers), he asserted: "The common sense of mankind does but support a conclusion thus forced upon us by analogical considerations." There was, in short, a "parallel to instances which happen daily" in the phenomenon of the development of Christian doctrine.

Especially, however, were such "parallels" to be found in the history of ideas. The first chapter of the *Essay* on development bore the title, "On the Development of Ideas," and in it Newman repeatedly sought to ground his own theory of doctrinal development in a generalized theory of how ideas are formed and grow. The very definition of development that Newman offered, and on which he based the balance of his argument in the book, appeared near the beginning of chapter one and applies not only to doctrine, but to all ideas. "This process, whether it be longer or shorter in time, by which the aspects of an idea are brought into consistency and form, I call its development, being the germination and maturation of some truth or apparent truth on a larger mental field." It was as true of Christian doctrine as of other fields of thought (and of other fields of thought as much as of Christian doctrine) that "time is necessary for the full comprehension and perfection of great ideas," for such was "the nature of the human mind." As "all great ideas"—including the divine right of kings, stoicism, utilitarianism, and free trade—developed, so did Christianity. And just as all living ideas—right or wrong, so long as they "live in men's minds"—did not remain in the mind of their recipient, but moved out into society to become public, so, too, it had been with Christianity.

Despite such parallels with philosophical and political ideas, Newman was well aware of living in "an intellectual age" in which, as he observed, "the human intellect is busy, and thought so fertile, and opinion so manifold"—a time, above all, of rapid change and development in the natural sciences. Hence it is especially instructive to pay closest attention, among the many kinds of analogy he drew in support of his case, to his use of the natural sciences for corroboration. "It is the rule of creation," he propounded, "or rather of the phenomena which it presents, that life passes on to its termination by a gradual, imperceptible course of change." Therefore he could adapt the method of the traditional "proof from design" (which, you will recall, Darwin knew from William Paley's book on *Evidences of Christianity*, and which was also Newman's source) to the presentation of the case for development. Much more profoundly, he was beginning already in 1845 to adapt to his argument the very question of the nature of proof and evidence. Not only was it true of scientific theories like gravitation, no less than of religious beliefs, that they were taken for granted simply because they were generally received, but (his phrase) "that which is considered to constitute a sufficient proof of truths in physical science" provided illumination for Newman's way of arguing his case. Already in the introduction, just after bringing the term *development* into his exposition for the first time, he met, head on, the possible objection that this was "an hypothesis to account for a difficulty." Of course it was, he freely granted; so, too, "are the various explanations given by astronomers from Ptolemy to Newton of the apparent motions of the heavenly bodies." Elsewhere, on the basis of a familiar passage from Francis Bacon, Newman sought to differentiate between those sciences that were susceptible of "strict investigation" in which "facts are present . . . [and] are submitted to the senses" for testing and empirical verification, and those sciences, such as "history, antiquities, political science, ethics, metaphysics, and theology," where a different system of verification obtained. Above all, in his *Apologia Pro Vita Sua* and then in what is perhaps his most profound book, the *Grammar of Assent,* Newman would carry the analysis a great deal further, to argue, on the basis of what he came to call the "illative sense," that probability was in fact all that was possible, but also all that was necessary, for the "proof" of the Christian faith.

As his reference to "a sufficient proof of truths in physical science" suggests, Newman was ready to draw analogies between his theory of development and the physical sciences. I have already quoted his statement that heresies "determine in what way the current is setting and the rate at which it flows." In an earlier discussion, he took up a familiar analogy, one that is particularly beloved of Protestant theologians in their assertion of the supremacy of Scripture over tradition. "the stream is clearest nearest to the spring." Newman replied by extending the metaphor to suggest that in the case of "the history of a philosophy or belief," the opposite of this maxim obtained —the stream of an idea is "more equable, and purer, and stronger, when its bed has become deep, and broad, and full." Similarly, he cited the first book of Euclid as an illustration of his distinction between doctrines and principles, which had a parallel in the distinction between Euclid's definitions and his axioms or postulates. He excluded "mathematical developments" from his purview, because, he said, they were of a different order in the use of the word *development.* They were different from "doctrines and views which relate to man."

It was, then, not with physics or mathematics, but rather with the biological sciences that Newman felt most comfortable in his search for appropriate metaphors and analogies to describe the development of doctrine. As I have already indicated, the language of "fecundity" and of "generation" came to his mind in the interpretation of how doctrines came from principles, albeit with the warning that "this analogy must not be strained." That's the warning one always uses with analogies that one is afraid are going to blow up in one's face. At the very end of the *Essay of Development,* the troubling realities of deformation and reformation in the church appeared as "the temporary cessation of . . . activity" in sleep and the "restoration" of awakening. More often, the language of disease and health was the appropriate way to deal with these realities. One of the most sustained expositions of an analogy in the *Essay* came at a crucial transition in which Newman introduces his seven "notes of a genuine development" that set it apart from a corruption. If there are many developments, how do you identify which ones are authentic? Except, of course, for the fact that authority has so identified them, how else can you identify them? Diseases, he says, might in some sense be "natural," and yet they are no less destructive. *Corruption* is a term he takes from medicine to describe that stage at which a body has reached its perfection, is now losing its vigor and powers of nutrition, of assimilation, and of self-reparation. When that happened to the church and its doctrines, there was corruption, the breaking up of life preparatory to its termination. But, of course, that had not happened.

The most adaptable analogy of all was, of course, that of growth, of "germination and maturation," and most of all, of the progress of human life from childhood to maturity. What is young differs from what is mature. The later form of a doctrine differs from its early one. Small are a baby's limbs, a youth's are larger, and yet they are the same. From Newman's fondness for these and many, many other biological analogies, it seems clear he could not have found a more fitting paradigm for what he was trying to say about the development of Christian doctrine as a "change" that was "real and perceptible, yet without substantial loss."

In fact, the only paradigm that would in at least some ways have been even more fitting would have been that of the evolution of a species. For in that paradigm he would have found both external forces and what he called the "innate power of expansion," both authentic continuity and genuine change, which he claimed to discern in the careers of various ideas. Yet, neither in the original edition of 1845 nor in the revised edition of 1878, nineteen years after the *Origin of Species*, did evolution, even as a term, provide Newman with such a paradigm. What the author of the foreword to the most recent edition (1960) of Newman's *Essay* wrote remains true today: "even after Darwin's work had been published Newman made no comment on it. It may well be that Newman's own discovery of evolution as an historical force was a personal insight without much dependence on others. Who can say?"

Who can say indeed? Yet, although that is where our present historical understanding of the relation between "emanation, evolution, and development" in the "legacy of Darwin" must leave the matter, it is not the last word to be said on the relation between Being and Becoming. Rather, that last word must come from Newman himself. Describing what he called "development in ideas" (yet surely thinking not only of the development of doctrine, but of his own development), he formulated an epigram that still summarizes, without a wasted word, the new discovery to which he and Darwin, in separate fields and independently of each other, as far as we can tell, had both come in 1844 when Darwin wrote his "sketch of the conclusions" and Newman wrote his "general view":

In a higher world it is otherwise, but here below to live is to change, and to be perfect is to have changed often.

And, we would have to add from both, it is to go on changing.

Appendix A:
Stephen Jay Gould's Extemporaneous Comments on Evolutionary Hope and Realities

Much of our evolutionary thinking reflects some of the deepest biases of Western thought, four of which I'd like to discuss because I think they've been central in our misunderstanding of evolution and in our unwillingness to come to terms with Darwin's world. When we understand the nature of these pervasive biases of Western thought, I think we will also understand better what kind of a revolutionary Darwin was and why even the millions of people who were quite content to acknowledge the fact of evolution itself found his theory so difficult to accept.

I think the first of these four great biases is progressionism, or the idea that the history of change on the earth is somehow a history of progressive alteration leading to that last great product of the creation—namely, us—and that if we were to look at evolution, it would have ladderlike properties of progressive, cosmic advance. Now, linked to that bias is, secondly, a general preference to see progressive changes as being gradual in nature, so that progress is achieved through a long and laborious set of steps up that ladder. A third important bias is determinism, by which I mean the general idea that events have causes and are somehow "right," so that chance as an agent of change in the world is banned. We're very uncomfortable with that notion; we remain so. And the fourth great bias is what I call adaptationism, by which I do not narrowly mean Darwin's theory of natural selection by any means, which is in part about adaptation. By adaptationism, I have in mind the larger world view that things "fit." Organisms fit in their environments, and environments fit into the earth, and the earth is somehow right. Now clearly, all those four views—progressionism, gradualism, determinism, and adaptationism—go together to form a set of comforts and hopes, to form a world that we would like to accept, one indeed in which we would feel quite comfortable.

I think I can illustrate all four of these biases from my favorite source of quotations in Western literature after the Bible—namely, Alexander Pope's *An Essay on Man,* which stands as a great document of eighteenth-century thought, the matrix of thought out of which our hopes about evolution have emerged. Let me then illustrate all of my four biases in the lines that form the end of the first part of that work.

First, on the subject of progress and gradualism in invoking the old theme of the chain of being, Pope talks about the arrangement of organisms in a hierarchy from amoeba to man. And he writes in heroic couplets:

> Far as Creation's ample range extends,
> The scale of sensual, mental pow'rs ascends:
> Mark how it mounts, so Man's imperial race,
> From the green myriads in the people grass:

And then talking more explicitly about the chain of being, Pope writes:

> Vast chain of being, which from God began,
> Natures aethereal, human, angel, man,

> Beast, bird, fish, insect! what no eye can see,
> No glass can reach! from Infinite to thee, . . .
> From Nature's chain whatever link you strike,
> Tenth or ten thousandth, breaks the chain alike.

In this couplet, you can see the political usages of biases and world views—that every creature and every human being has his appropriate status on the earth, and that the poor peasant, the ten-thousandth link, is as essential and where he ought to be as is the king on the first link. In the very next lines, Pope goes on to invoke, in the usual metaphor, what the world would be like if determinism did not rule the cosmos. And he invokes that equation of randomness with chaos which is so fundamentally incorrect, but so often done:

> Let Earth unbalanc'd from her orbit fly,
> Planets and Suns run lawless thro' the sky,
> Let ruling Angels from their spheres be hurl'd,
> Being on being wreck'd, and world on world,
> Heav'n's whole foundations to their centre nod,
> And Nature tremble to the throne of God:

A little bit before, he talks about the adaptationist view that things are fundamentally right and in their proper positions on this earth in a wonderful set of lines where he says that although some men may be dissatisfied with the acuity of their senses, those senses are apportioned to our proper status. He starts:

> Why has not Man a microscopic eye?
> For this plain reason, Man is not a Fly.

That requires a little exegesis—it was believed, incorrectly, at that time that the compound eyes of flies and other insects allowed them to see microscopically the small objects of their dimensions. That's wrong, of course.

> Say what the use, were finer optics giv'n,
> T'inspect a mite, not comprehend the heav'n?

And then talking about touch:

> Or touch, if tremblingly alive all o'er,
> To smart and agonize at ev'ry pore?

Then my favorite line about smell:

> Or quick effluvia darting thro' the brain,
> Die of a rose in aromatic pain?

And then on sound,

> If nature thunder'd in his op'ning ears,
> And stunn'd him with the music of the spheres,
> How would he wish that Heav'n had left him still
> The whisp'ring Zephyr, and the purling rill?

And finally, the famous lines at the end of his first epistle of *An Essay on Man,* where all the biases are brought together and united again with the political point:

> All Nature is but Art, unknown to thee;
> All Chance, Direction, which thou canst not see;
> All Discord, Harmony, not understood;
> All partial Evil, universal Good:
> And, spite of Pride, in erring Reason's spite,
> One truth is clear, "Whatever IS, is RIGHT."

Now that is the matrix of our hopes, the matrix of the biases that Darwin's theory challenges. Modern evolutionary theory leads us to question all four of these biases, and I think that this is largely why it has been so difficult for us to accept it.

Darwin tried to do two very difficult things in his life: first, to establish the fact of evolution, an endeavor in which he was abundantly successful; and second, to propose a theory called the theory of natural selection to explain its mechanism. I'm talking about the implications of the theory of natural selection. Darwin was very explicit about these two very separate goals. He wrote, for example, in the *Descent of Man:* "I had two distinct objects in view. Firstly to show that species had not been separately created and secondly that natural selection had been the chief agent of change." The mere fact of evolution is hard enough for many people to swallow, but there are congenial versions of evolutionary mechanisms that support all four of the great biases that I've identified. For example, Lamarckism is an evolutionary theory that accepts progressionism, gradualism, determinism, and adaptationism as part of its mechanisms, and I think this is one of the main reasons why Lamarckian evolutionary theories remained so popular long after the genetic rationale for them had disappeared— and why they keep recurring. They match our hopes and what we would like to believe. But Darwinian theory, the theory of natural selection, attacks those biases. Darwin's personal views attacked two of them, and the expansions and extensions of Darwinian theory that we recognize today attack all four of them.

Natural selection is not a theory of random change. It does incorporate randomness, but not to produce change. This is another aspect of natural selection theory that's widely misunderstood. Natural selection theory is a two-part theory. Randomness is called upon to produce the raw material, to produce the variation upon which natural selection acts; but evolutionary change is the result of natural selection working upon this random pool of raw material and selecting out the adaptive component thereof. Therefore, Darwinism is not a theory of random change; it calls upon randomness only to produce raw material. Yet so great is our fear of randomness as an agent of change that many people reject Darwinism based on this misunderstanding. Arthur Koestler says it all the time—that Darwinism is a theory of random change and therefore we have to reject it because the world is ordered. Well, first of all, you can produce a lot of order within random systems, and second of all, Darwinism is not a theory of random change. It calls upon randomness for raw material only.

Darwin himself rejected two of the four biases directly—

progressionism and adaptationism. And, as I just said, he challenged determinism halfway. But modern evolutionary theory challenges all four of the biases. There are many trends in evolutionary theory at all levels that are calling upon randomness as a source of evolutionary change, not replacing natural selection, but expanding the range of evolutionary mechanisms that can account for transformation, not merely for raw material. At the level of genes, the theory of neutral mutations argues that a large number of genetic changes in evolutionary lineages may occur without reference to phenotypic adaptation. At the level of species, we're getting many theories arguing that at least the initial step in speciation—the attainment of reproductive isolation—may be achieved not for reasons of adaptation, but by essentially accidental chromosomal changes that render a small group reproductively isolated from others. Now that group will not ultimately be successful unless it later develops subsidiary adaptations. I don't mean that adaptation will play no role in the formation of new species, but it may not be all that happens. At the level of macroevolution or major patterns in the history of life, another set of studies shows that random processes can produce much of the high degree of order that we see in the fossil record. Random systems do produce apparent order. Think of coin flipping—you get ten heads in a row every once in a while.

What, then, specifically of us and our evolution? I think the most curious thing about the history of attempts to explain human evolution is our general unwillingness to extend to ourselves the consequences that we're sometimes willing to accept for the rest of nature.

There are two tendencies we use to try to preserve our hopes and biases, at least for us. The first strategy I like to call the "Strategy of the Picket Fence." Under that strategy, you apply courageously to all of nature a set of naturalistic evolutionary explanations, and then you make some special exception for us at the last minute. This is what Wallace did for the human brain. It's what Charles Lyell did, for example, in arguing that the world was in steady state, did not show progress, but that man and man alone represents an imposition of the moral order, progressively placed on earth at the end of time.

The second strategy, quite opposite, is called anthropocentricism. Here you do put man in nature; you don't try to establish the picket fence and make us separate; you put man squarely into nature. But, in a crazy reversal of causality, you see nature as existing for and directed towards us, as though nature for four and a half billion years existed only to cough us up at the end of time. A powerful representation of this theme in the last twenty years is the movie *2001*, with its finalistic account of human evolution and progress.

In my view, one should talk neither of the absolute separation of the picket fence nor of the total immersion of the anthropocentric vision. You have to look at some middle way. Human beings are special. All species are special in some way in nature. Though we are special, however, we are the accidental result of an unplanned process and we may not see all of nature through us. We are special, but not apart. The ways in which we are special have had profound consequences for the nature of our planet, particularly through the agency of consciousness that we have unleashed on the earth. As Peter Medawar once said so well, this new process of cultural evolution is Lamarckian in form; you do have the transmission of acquired characters from one generation to another. What we learn, we pass on to our offspring, and the Lamarckian system accelerates evolution at such an enormous pace that the attainment of this Lamarckian style through human cultural evolution has caused a true rupture in the history of our earth.

Secondly, as a result of the unleashing of consciousness and cultural evolution, the earth is changing, due to our agency, at an unprecedented rate. Just look out an airplane window. Nonetheless, it's all an accident in a larger sense. We are the fragile result of an enormous concatenation of improbabilities, not the predictable product of any definite process.

Let me just close by giving you one example of the concatenation of improbabilities. As you know, there was a great extinction 65 million years ago. The dinosaurs that had dominated the earth—at least, the realms of large-bodied vertebrates—for 100 million years became extinct. We've only had 65 million years since then. There's no reason to think that if the dinosaurs hadn't become extinct, we and other mammals would have evolved as we did. Mammals had already lived for 100 million years. Most of the history of mammals is not the history of their success since the extinction of dinosaurs, but rather the history of 100 million years as small creatures living in the interstices of a dinosaur's world. Had the dinosaurs continued, I think mammals would still be small creatures living in these interstices, and *Triceratops* might have been running around here rather than all you listening to us.

Now what's the cause of the Cretaceous extinction? Who knows? It's probably very complex, but most of you are aware that within the last years a very serious theory (probably correct in my view) argues that at least a strong contributing factor in the Cretaceous extinction was the impact of some large extraterrestrial body upon the earth. Now suppose that's true? And suppose that without it, the dinosaurs might not have died. What's more, we know of only one lineage of primates, a little form called *Purgatorius,* that lived before this potential asteroid hit. Suppose this lineage had become extinct? Primates would not have evolved again. Many lineages of mammals did become extinct. The impact of a large extraterrestrial body, that greatest of all improbabilities, may well have been the *sine qua non* of our existence. And hundreds of other historically contingent improbabilities were also essential parts of human evolution.

Now, finally, lest you think I'm trying to give you a pessimistic message, I don't see it that way. I view optimistically everything I'm saying. I am saying that there are no direct answers in nature to our hopes and to our moral dilemmas; but I think that's fine. I don't think you're supposed to look to the facts of nature for the answers to moral dilemmas. I think that's a job for human intellect to construct for itself. That's the job of humanistic scholars; it's a job for all of us as human beings, not the job of scientists to find it in nature. Isn't this an optimistic message for starting the search?

Appendix B:
Conversations at Nobel XVIII,
"Darwin's Legacy"

CHAIRMAN: I have a question for Mr. Wilson from the audience. Violent relationships and child abuse have been said to be present in about 50 percent of the nuclear family units in the United States right now. Is this culturally or individually adaptive?

WILSON: Well, I don't know. I don't know all the circumstances and the data on child abuse and how it's defined and the like. But to try to shed some light on the question, because it is so important, one can observe that a very large percentage of the cases of child abuse are by stepparents, and that would be, in some contexts, genetically adaptive. It's been documented recently that infanticide is widespread in the animal kingdom up to and including some of the primates, and that this kind of aggression is typically associated with the invasion of unrelated adults who then become parents themselves and whose offspring enjoy the resources of the newly acquired territory. It has been argued back and forth as to whether this phenomenon has relevance for the human case, whether there might be some propensity to be less protective of or more abusive to children that are not directly related to the stepparent. Here again, we are talking not about absolutely determined characters, but about propensities that have to be measured as the probabilities of response in different situations. At the very least, the genetic adaptation hypothesis should be pursued to provide a fuller background for understanding the problem of child abuse and to predict where the worst cases will occur.

AUDIENCE: Mr. Wilson, can you briefly describe how your research on social insects led you to considerations of the relationship among human heredity, behavior, and culture?

WILSON: How did I end up sitting here? Well, I was an entomologist for almost all my life until the 1960s, when I saw a need to bring together a synthesis of information on social insects (ants, bees, wasps, and termites) because no such work had been written in fifty years, and the field was in disarray. Young people couldn't get into the subject because there was no central place for them to get basic information. When I wrote the book *The Insect Societies,* I tried to put the subject on a foundation of population biology. Then I saw that this could also be done for the rest of the animal kingdom. With a lot of work and the help of colleagues, I wrote *Sociobiology: The New Synthesis.* I added two chapters on the applications of this relatively new field to human behavior. At that point, I thought I was going to go back to zoology, but the response to the human chapters, both negative and positive, was so great that it drew me on into several more years of research on human behavior, and three more books. Now, at last—I think—I'm getting back more into social insects.

MEDAWAR: I was delighted and fascinated by what Steve Gould was saying. I really didn't prepare myself to comment on it very coherently, but I'd like to draw him out on the subject of the great chain of being. I think a case can be made for saying that the greatest cultural shock ever experienced by mankind was the discovery in the fifteenth and sixteenth centuries of the manlike apes, the anthropoid apes. The great voyages of discovery brought back scary talk of the existence of manlike apes; apes such as Linneaus himself put into the same taxon, *anthropomorpha*, as man. Orangutangs in Southeast Asia, chimps and such like in East Africa. Now you would have thought that the discovery of these half-animal, half-men would have most profoundly scared and upset people—this evidence of a link between animals and man. And yet the literature of that period contains no evidence of any such frightened references. The explanation put to me by a learned fellow who was interested in this period and these problems is that the notion of a great scale of being had already entered so deeply into the culture, that it seemed almost natural that manlike apes should exist. There was a niche there, a visible gap, and it had to be filled in, if the great scale of being was to be a complete one, all the way from the simplest, most elementary creatures through to man and perhaps even to God. And if it is true that we are so deeply informed by the notion of the great scale of being, then this must take away a little bit from the impact Darwin had upon his first readers. I'd like Dr. Gould to respond to this point if he thinks there is any substance in it.

GOULD: That's a very interesting point. It's quite true that Linneaus included several subspecies within the genus *Homo*, one of which was *Homo troglydytes*, based on faulty travelers' reports of what we now know to be the great apes. I think that the explanation given by your "learned friend" is correct in the sense that, accompanying the chain of being theory was the notion that there would be absolute and complete continuity, and that any apparent gaps, empirical gaps that existed in the world, were really just the result of a lack of discovery. I will cite one example, even give you another quotation from Pope. The greatest gap, of course, occurred between man and the angels or man and God. And even if you could fill in everything from amoeba to man on earth, what would bridge that gap if there were a true chain of being leading up to God? Now Immanuel Kant's answer to that was that there would be superior beings on other planets. And if we could find them, they would fill in the gaps, because the chain of being cannot have lacunae. Pope actually writes about this in the *Essay on Man.* He imagines the people on Jupiter observing Isaac Newton and being amazed that a mere mortal, inferior human on earth, could think of such things, and he writes,

> Superior beings, when of late they saw
> A mortal man unfold all nature's law
> Admired such wisdom in an earthly shape
> And showed a Newton, as we show an ape.

I think what was radical about evolutionary thought, with respect to the chain of being, was that it "temporalized" the chain, in Lovejoy's words. The chain of being as it existed for Pope and Newton was static. God had chosen to create this way without gaps, and there was no physical or genealogical connection among the steps of the chain. When you have the notion of genealogical connection, the amoeba is actually an ancestor, not just the lowest stage on the created scale. And of course then, with Darwinism, you don't even have the chain anymore; you have this accidentally constructed luxuriant, tangled bank—the branching bush.

AUDIENCE: What do you think of the theory proposed by Arnold C. Brackman's book, *A Delicate Arrangement?* Perhaps Darwin may have cheated Wallace?

STONE: The story of Charles Darwin and Wallace is a very interesting one. Darwin had been working on his book, *The Origin of Species,* for twenty solid years and had achieved a two-thousand-page, rambunctious, and not brilliantly organized manuscript. He had no intention of publishing it during his lifetime because he knew that, as in the words of Milton, "all hell would break loose." So, in his will, he bequeathed four hundred pounds to be paid to one of his friends, either Joseph Hooker or Charles Lyell, to edit this two-thousand-page manuscript down to about four to six hundred pages. At this point, he received in the mail, from a young man by the name of Wallace, a seven-page article which was exactly the same as his theory of the origin of species. He was amazed and confounded and didn't know what to do with himself or the manuscript. He called Joseph Hooker and Lyell out to Downe House. They came and read the Wallace manuscript. The script was almost word for word what was in the Darwin two thousand pages, though there was no way Wallace could have known what Darwin was writing. Darwin wanted the Wallace paper read at the Linnean Society by itself, to give Wallace precedence, but his two friends said no. We will, they said, if you will first extract a number of pages from your vast manuscript, edit them down to seven pages, and allow the two articles to be read side by side at the Linnean Society. And so they were, but they attracted no attention whatsoever, not even a discussion, which certainly burdened Darwin quite a lot. As far as the controversy is concerned, let me first quote Wallace. Wallace said many times during his life, "Darwin is the originator of the concept of the origin of species and natural selection." The purpose of the author [of *A Delicate Arrangement*] was, in my mind, to create a scandal, a bit of sensationalism, which would sell the book.

GOULD: I might just add one word to that. I agree entirely that the book by Brackman doesn't even treat the primary principle of natural selection. All he's talking about in his accusations is that after Darwin received Wallace's letter from Malaysia, there may have been some hanky-panky going on concerning a totally different principle called the principle of divergence, which is not an unimportant aspect of evolutionary theory. Yet in the hoopla surrounding the book, it was widely reported in the press—and, I think, almost half-encouraged at least by the publishers—that somehow here was a charge that Darwin was a plagiarist. And yet the one thing that's absolutely undeniable is that the primary importance of Darwin's theory is the principle of natural selection. Now Darwin developed this principle and wrote it down in manuscript in 1838 when Wallace was a teenager, and Brackman says so, of course, but he buries the information in a paragraph. With respect to the fundamental feature—Darwin's theory of natural selection—there can't be any question of Darwin's priority. Just look at Wallace's ontogeny and where he was, and as Mr. Stone says, Wallace's own statements during his own lifetime gave the lie to that notion.

AUDIENCE: Mr. Gould, you expressed eloquently what you believe the world is not and that it is "a set of historically contingent accidents." What's the difference between a world composed of random accidents and chaos?

GOULD: To me, the word *chaos* in the vernacular means horribly confused, fearful, etcetera. But I think the basic principle of history is that you don't have, given its enormous complexity, a system that yields complete predictability— that's what we mean by accident. Accident, to me, doesn't have the vernacular connotation of chaos. It means we have a series of events so complex, each so dependent upon prior history, that we cannot have the kind of predictability that you get in the so-called hard or physical sciences where, when hydrogen and oxygen came together under certain circumstances a billion years ago, they made water, just as they do now and as they will in a billion years. This doesn't make the so-called historical sciences less scientific; it gives them a different style. Their style is explanation after events happen; it's not a prediction. By accident, I merely mean that the actual result which we see is a series of historically contingent occurrences. I'll give one example. You hear me in part through a series of three bones called the hammer, anvil, and stirrup, or the malleus, incus, and stapes. The evolutionary history of two of those bones, the malleus and incus, is fascinating. In your ancestors, some 400 million years ago, they were gill-support bones of ancestral, jawless fishes. They moved forward in the first jawed vertebrates to form bones within the jaw; and those two bones, the malleus and incus, were in fact—and still are in reptiles—the articulation bones of the upper and lower jaws. In the evolution of mammals, they then passed into the middle ear. Now who, 400 million years ago, no matter how good an engineer he might have been, would have predicted after looking at that primitive jawless fish, "Aha, I *know* through the principles of physics and engineering, in 300 million years, those two bones are going to be in the inner ear of some hairy creature." You couldn't make that prediction. After it happens, you can explain it and trace its course. That's what we mean by historical contingency as accidental. It's the fundamental feature of historical science. It does not imply chaos; it merely records the importance of history.

AUDIENCE: At the conclusion of his lecture, Professor Gould suggested that we should not look to the scientific study of nature for the solution to ethical dilemmas, yet Professor Wilson concluded that science must tell us what we are and, hence, where we ought to go as human beings. What is the relation between the scientific study of nature and the solution to ethical problems?

WILSON: As evolutionary biology has deepened, it has been possible to predict changes in small ensembles of genes over short periods of time, and our knowledge of adaptation and natural constraints has steadily improved. I believe that as we begin to see the relation between the constraints in our minds and evolutionary change, and come up with better explanations of where our species came from and why culture has certain central traits and variations, we will be able to judge with a good deal more competence which courses of action are easier to take and which are difficult or even dangerous. I foresee science, biology in particular, and evolutionary biology most particularly, as serving in an advisory capacity—not making the ultimate ethical decisions, but counseling on the most prudent courses of action. We have to appreciate that some cultural shifts would cause a radical alteration of society and have a devastating effect on the individual psyche. Let me just give you one example: incest. Until fairly recently, there still was some kind of argument going on about whether incest avoidance and the incest taboo are natural, or whether they were simply the last residues of the old cultural order—so that breaking them would be the final step in sexual liberation. There have actually been serious proposals by a few philosophers and others that perhaps we should reduce or abolish the incest taboos and perhaps be healthier for it. Without going into the substantial evidence that has accumulated from genetics, anthropology, cognitive psychology, and sociobiology, let me say that we can answer that question definitively right now. In no sense of the word is incest avoidance to be regarded as anything but very natural. Lowering the guard —that is, reducing or breaking the taboo, and hence increasing the level of inbreeding—would result in terrible genetic damage. Furthermore, to encourage incest is likely to cause substantial psychic damage due to the deep inhibitions that develop automatically in young children. So with this kind of information, in various categories of behavior and social arrangements, biologists should be in a better position to join social scientists in advising on ethical guidelines. I am not quite prepared yet to take the final step and say abolish the distinction between *is* and *ought.* But I do believe we will be able to make far superior decisions on the most difficult ethical problems through an improved scientific knowledge of human nature.

GOULD: Wilson says he's just about ready to abolish the distinction between *is* and *ought*. I've always supported that old philosophical chestnut. (Remember, a chestnut's a chestnut because there's a strong element of good argument in it.) The way in which the world *is* cannot prescribe morality, which is fundamentally a question of *ought*. I think that's fundamentally a sound position. On the other hand, just as a matter of common sense, one always wants to know as much as one can about the way the world is. It would be very difficult, even though it's ethically perfectly logical and reasonable, to try to advocate an ethic that's so out of accord with basic human biology that there will be enormous pain and suffering if we institute it. For instance, if I say that the only good person is someone who, in flapping his arms, can fly from here to the other end of the room, then we're going to have a terrible psychological burden because none of us can do it. I think it's good common sense to know as much as possible about the nature of the world to help inform ourselves when we try to construct an ethic. But I don't think this means that learning more about biological constraints comes closer to abolishing the distinction between actuality and our own assessment of propriety.

AUDIENCE: Do you accept Lovejoy's explanation of the connection between human sexuality and bipedalism?

LEAKEY: I think that it's one of those things that is going to be extremely difficult to prove. The bones tell you nothing about sexuality; the bones tell you nothing about diet. We simply know from the bones that there was a certain moment in time when an ape became bipedal. I think it's a hypothesis in the strict sense of the word, and it's worth looking at, but I don't accept it as the only possible explanation. I think it's most likely that bipedalism is related to a dietary shift rather than to a reproductive shift, but then diet and reproduction are intricately linked and so one must be a little careful on that issue.

GOULD: If you survey the history of guesswork explanations in the adaptationist mode, they bear an uncanny resemblance to societal trends in general. When we lived in a much more sexist age, virtually all the adaptive speculations about the origin of anything human never considered women at all. Women were home in the cave cooking and everything had to do with men hunting. Now that we're a little more sensitive to issues of sexism, a hypothesis comes up which talks about the importance of women gathering, with men hunting, and of the monogamous family unit. It's a hypothesis for our age! That doesn't make it any more plausible, though it might well be right, but its popularity arises because it resonates with our age, not because there's any particular fossil evidence going for it.

AUDIENCE: Does acceptance of the theory of evolution rule out a belief in God the Creator or in any supernatural being?

MEDAWAR: It is I who shall have to answer that, because it was I who said if Soapy Sam had not lost the opportunity to inject a little rational piety into the evolutionary debate, he might have said that it didn't really matter whether or not God had gone to the trouble and expense of creating each individual organism as a separate creative act. We would perhaps have admired him more if what God had created was the general setup which made evolution possible—if he had, as it were, set the machine rolling. That would, in a way, have been the remarkable and wonderful thing to do. I think that the answer can rest only with faith. If you believe in God the Creator, then this is the way in which he might have gone about it. But as this is a matter of belief, there can be no logical discussion of it. Empirical evidence does not bear upon it at all. Science has only to do with empirical evidence. It does not deal with matters of faith, except so far as empirical evidence may help to explain how we come to hold certain faiths and not others, and have certain kinds of expectations and not others. There is no answer to that question that I could give as a scientist.

GOULD: As a purely empirical point, there must be compatibility, because although there are many scientists who are atheists, thousands of scientists hold a belief in a personal God—and they hold the same views about evolution as those of us who may be atheists do. Such a situation can only arise because there is no incompatibility, through lack of context; they are entirely separate domains.

LEAKEY: I would simply like to add complete support for what is being said. I've known many friends and colleagues who are deeply religious, not only in the Christian religion but in others, who also happen to be extremely good scientists. I don't think there's any question at all that they are compatible, but they are different issues: one is based on faith and one is based on empirical evidence. I think it's very sad that we continue to see an attempt made by a minority element to bring science and religion into further conflict.

AUDIENCE: Sir Peter, there's a question that I think falls well within what you were talking about. If any hypothesis falls short of proof, how does one decide between rival hypotheses? Are there degrees of conformity or falsifiability? What criteria does one use when one is seeking advice?

MEDAWAR: Are there degrees of acceptability of hypotheses? Yes, of course there are. All I'm saying is that there is no logical process by which we can accept the truth of an hypothesis as a matter of apodictic certainty—that is, arrive at a demonstration so decisive and ostensibly so complete that critical questioning is no longer possible. Every hypothesis can be criticized, and many of them are modified as a consequence of the criticism. No hypothesis is exempt from critical scouting. But the kind of hypothesis we accept in science, according to the widely accepted view of Karl Popper—and of Kant also, incidentally—is that a scientific hypothesis is one that is in principle falsifiable. We must be able to think up an experiment or observation which in principle could falsify it. That is what makes a hypothesis a scientific one as distinct from a mere whimsical invention. And this is one of the embarrassments about Darwinism. It's too glib. It's too difficult to think of any evolutionary phenomenon which couldn't be explained by that glib form of words trotted out of Professor Minchin about the forms of the spicules of sponges. This is why Karl Popper said Darwinism was almost metaphysical in character. As to the hypothesis of evolution by natural selection, it is too difficult to think of a way of testing it critically. Critically means with the possibility of falsifying. I'm damned if I know. Do you, Steve?

GOULD: Oh, I can think of ways that would falsify Darwinism on a very broad scale, but they won't serve to give us enough confidence to call it a hypothesis sufficiently well confirmed that we are compelled to believe it. For example, during the nineteenth century, we knew little about mechanisms of heredity. If it turned out that mechanisms of heredity, when elucidated, allowed for a Lamarckian mode of transmission, it would have effectively disproved Darwinism—not that Darwinism wouldn't have operated, rather that, if the Lamarckian system worked, it would operate so quickly that natural selection could not have been quantitatively important. Now it didn't work out that way, and therefore the elucidation of the mechanism of heredity did favor, by the elimination of lots of alternatives, the Darwinian mechanism.

AUDIENCE: How can so highly integrated a process like expansion of the cerebral hemispheres or attainment of uprightness have evolved by a punctuation event?

GOULD: First of all, the theory of punctuated equilibrium is not a theory of sudden transformation of the phenotype in its entirety. That's a kind of willful distortion that creationists particularly like to make as a rhetorical foray in equating punctuated equilibrium with a caricature of what's called the theory of macromutation, or the theory of hopeful monsters. Even Richard Goldschmidt, who was a believer in a much more rapid, single-generation transition, didn't imagine a sudden origin of an entirely integrated new structure, but merely the origin of certain key characters about which slower adaptation would have to equilibrate later. In any case, the theory of punctuated equilibrium is not about that. The theory of punctuated equilibrium is a theory about macroevolutionary patterns and about what causes trends in evolution. It argues that large-scale changes in evolution are brought about, not through a slow and steady transformation within lineages, but by accumulated events of speciation; therefore, if upright posture did arise in a speciation event through the process of punctuated equilibrium, it would have been an ordinary speciation event that took thousands of years. I don't believe for a moment that upright posture arose in a single generation.

AUDIENCE: Any prospect for the advent of regeneration to replace lost limbs and/or organs soon?

MEDAWAR: This is totally irrelevant to the subject we are discussing. It doesn't matter; the answer is no. I think human beings will evolve further; they could in principle. My wife and I wrote a book on biology in which we described human beings as the "great amateurs among animals." They are perfectly well evolvable. There's nothing about a human being that commits him to any one particular kind of life. He has an open breeding system and a vast reserve of genetic variance. Human beings could evolve. When I was a tutor at Oxford—a pedagogic device in which one has a one-to-one relation with some hopeful youngster who is trying to learn biology—my pupil once asked, "Will human beings evolve into the possession of wings so that they can fly?" And bless me, my pupil had to raise his voice to make it heard over the sound of a passing airplane. He did not realize we can fly already, as we are also submarine animals, and animals that live in polar regions, and under the sea and on the tops of mountains. Since we can do all this already, why do you want to evolve actual physical organs, and genetically? We evolve through an entirely different and much more efficient process. We are flying animals, submarine animals, terrestrial animals. You name any faculty: we could or do possess it. In principle, everything is possible, can be done, if the intention to do it is resolute enough. And we do have artificial limbs already. I've got one myself. I'll show it to you for a donation to my research.

CHAIRMAN: First of all, are there any immediate responses on the part of the participants to Mr. Pelikan's address?

GOULD: Mr. Pelikan, the question of proper biological analogs is ever fascinating. However, I was very interested in two aspects of Cardinal Newman's work as expressed in your talk: first, that he uses the term *development,* and second, that he felt there was a kind of inevitability in correctness through change in the development of Christian thought. In early nineteenth-century England, the biological context of the word *development,* as indeed we use it today, was for ontogeny—that is, for individual growth. Now the interesting thing about ontogeny, or embryological development, is that because it is directed by a DNA program, it does have a correct or at least an average course of development; therefore, it was certainly a proper biological analog, if indeed Newman got it from biology. There is still the fundamental difference between ontogeny and phylogeny. That is why ontogeny, or the development of the individual, is an improper analog for understanding evolutionary change, which is not preprogrammed. On the subject of evolution itself, since the word meant so many things other than what

Darwin had in mind—it meant emanation, as you said, and it also meant progress to Herbert Spencer, for example— Darwin assiduously avoided the word. In *The Origin of Species*, he talks about "descent with modification," because his view of the contingent accidents of history and the unpredictability of the process precluded the vernacular sense of evolution. And I think it's only because the nineteenth century was so comfortable with the equation of organic change with progress that Spencer's usage took precedence and even Darwin bowed to it and started to use the term *evolution* to mean organic change by the late 1870s and 1880s.

AUDIENCE: Mr. Wilson, what does evolutionary theory tell us about the foundation of ethics and morality?

WILSON: The central question of ethical philosophy, I am convinced, and I believe that it should be of primary concern to theology as well, is whether or not ethical precepts originated entirely within the evolution of the human mind. Because if they did, it makes all the difference in the world. One could easily imagine wholly different ethical systems evolving in other species. In fact, it's difficult in thought experiments not to imagine it happening that way. For example, if termites had somehow managed to ascend 100 million years ago to the pinnacle that human beings now occupy, if they came to weigh ten kilograms, with a growing neocortex and a rational apparatus developing on top of all the termite passions and mode of life, we would find them rationally explaining an ethical system with myths, legends, cultural heroes, sacred literature, and a termite God profoundly different from our own. Their theologians would advance, as absolute moral guidelines, a sacred caste system, cannibalism glorified, personal reproduction a sin in the worker castes, territorial war proper, darkness preferred to light, pheromonal song, and so on. The termite God would be terrifying to the human mind, but extremely congenial to the termite mind.

Only a few ethical philosophers have come to grips with this severest and most troubling of Darwin's legacies. We have to ask again whether or not morality might indeed be ultimately relativistic—or if there is something more. Recently, Robert Nozick, in his book *Philosophical Explanations,* conceded that the evolutionary analysis from sociobiology might be correct. But if it is correct, he said, it does not *dis*prove the existence outside the human mind of a set of absolute ethical precepts which the human species might be tracking by genetic and cultural means. And the analogy he used, which seemed to me very weak, was that there exist certain laws of numerosity employed by human beings that appear to exist outside human evolution and which we put adventitiously to use in mathematical theorems and a good deal of physical science. Is it not possible, he asked, that there also exist fundamental ethical precepts which we are tracking? If that much is true, we have a basis for extrabiological origins of moral reasoning. But I am not sure the termites would agree.

A similar approach has recently been taken by Peter Singer in his book, *The Expanding Circle,* in which he says that, yes, maybe the evolutionary explanation is correct. But there is something else beyond which justifies a steadily enlarging concern for the whole human species and even other species. A nice thought. Well, I raise this question as the one I regard as absolutely fundamental; there is none more important. I think it should be the point of departure for a colloquy between philosophers, theologians, and scientists, because up until now the philosophers and theologians have not demonstrated the way to identify the extrahuman, absolute moral precepts that our species might be tracking in the course of its evolution, and about which we desperately need to have more information.

MEDAWAR: I should very much like it if Dr. Pelikan would enlarge what he was saying about Cudworth. I think Cudworth's great work is so mind-numbingly dull that I may have misread him. My view of Cudworth was that he was one of those fellows that believed in "cyclical progression." He believed in the alteration of decay and regeneration. He did not have a glimmering of what we now think of as evolution, and I wanted to be clear that you weren't saying that he had, Dr. Pelikan; or were you?

PELIKAN: On the contrary, I thought I said that he did not have our content in that word. What I was seeking to show, and using Cudworth together with More as the source for, is that the term came into the language for something quite different, for something *not* temporal in its understanding, not sequential—but, as you say, cyclical and, behind that, nontemporal. And that's what happens as the word through Spencer and others is adapted. This is the process of temporalization to which I referred. I was not in any sense claiming him for that understanding of evolution, but for quite the opposite.

AUDIENCE: Would you agree with the statement that the theory of evolution is a temporal interpretation of the infallible dogma of creation?

PELIKAN: There aren't anything except temporal interpretations of any truth. That's all we've got. We are temporal by nature, and therefore, any statement is conditioned, approximate, bound by its time. And so if, in speaking of an "infallible dogma of creation," one intends to mean that there's a nontemporal, eternally unrevised teaching which is available to us here within time, one is propounding a concept which I am afraid my mind can't encompass. So I would say that the Nicene Creed is a temporal interpretation of the infallible dogma of creation, and so is any other statement. What is one affirming when one affirms in one or another area of life? Also, in relation to Professor Wilson's comment, it's significant, I think, that creation is not presented in the Bible, or in Christian history, as a dogma. It's presented as a story, as a myth, and that myth is employed to make certain statements which cannot be made in any other way. Moreover, the use of that myth, in later biblical literature, is really quite spotty, and the use of the myth of the Fall, even less frequent. There is, as far as I know, between the story of the Fall of Adam and Eve in the third chapter of Genesis, and the use of the story of the Fall of Adam in the fifth chapter of the Epistle to the Romans, no reference to the Fall of Adam and Eve in all the discussions of sin throughout the rest of the Old Testament and New Testament, and no reference to it in the teachings of Jesus. Throughout those, both creation and sin are treated directly and not by way of some ancestor in whom we sinned or through whom we are created. Psalm 139 and various other biblical statements make it clear that I, who am the product of a process that can be described naturally, am, through that process, the creature of God. That's what the biblical doctrine of creation was intended to state. But having said that twenty-three years ago for Sol Tax at the centennial of the *Origin,* I wanted to go on to the other implications of the problem, and that's what I've done today.

MEDAWAR: Logically speaking, prior to the idea of evolution is the idea of change, and this is quite a novel idea in European thought. I wonder if Dr. Pelikan would like to put a date, plus or minus fifty years, to when the notion of change became commonplace. That is, the idea that the world will not be the same when a person dies as it was when he was born—that the world into which a man's children are born will be different than that into which he himself was born. This is a new and rather revolutionary idea. I wonder if Dr. Pelikan will give his assessment of when this change in thought came about.

PELIKAN: It comes about, as far as I can tell, Sir Peter, differently in different fields of human thought and endeavor. It is frequently employed and pointed out as part of a polemic.

One points out that an institution, a set of laws, a political structure, a church, or whatsoever, which one is attacking has changed; whereas, since truth abides and the best abides, I have not changed, so that the documentation of change by historians and polemicists is done, in the first instance, in a negative way. My friend Owen Chadwick at Cambridge has a wonderful book called *From Bossuet to Newman*, in which the history of the notion of change is the central theme. He concentrates on some of the issues I've been concentrating on here, although from a different perspective. My sense is that the change in political institutions was probably the most thoroughly documented as a consequence of the historical work of the seventeenth and, especially, the eighteenth centuries. People like Montesquieu and others were probably the ones, as far as I can tell, who were doing it, and, of course, in the English public it was made a question of major debate through Edward Gibbon.

AUDIENCE: How do you counteract the widespread movement to force public schools to teach about scientific creationism if they also teach about the theory of evolution?

GOULD: I think scientists were a little slow when the creationist movement first resurged in a large way about three years ago, if only because we were so incredulous. We thought this was an issue that had been settled long ago. An older colleague of mine wrote to Woodrow Wilson in 1919, and Wilson responded that he couldn't see how, in this day and age, anybody could doubt organic evolution anymore, even though the current occupant of that high office, on the stump before a moral majority crowd in Dallas a few years ago, publicly doubted it. Nonetheless, scientists were provoked into combat—and high school teachers particularly have borne the brunt—and now there have been a series of very successful moves against the pseudoscience of creation, so much that I think the tide of this particular battle has turned. As Reagan's right-wing social program begins to fail in many areas, creationism, which, politically, has its status as a part of that movement, begins to lose steam. The trial in Arkansas last December, *McLean* vs. *The Arkansas Board of Education,* was a resounding victory, not so much for the truth of evolution, as that wasn't being contested, but for the clear demonstration that creationism is nothing but a dogmatic, particularistic view of religion masquerading as science. That victory in Arkansas pretty thoroughly thwarted what was to have been the great year of legislative triumph for the creationist movement. Having passed their bills in two state legislatures the year before in Arkansas and Louisiana, last year was to be their year of great success, and the bill never got out of committee, as far as I know, in any other state. On the basis of the Arkansas decision, many battles at the level of local school boards have been won, and many local boards that had begun to teach creationism have now rescinded that. In the area of textbook publishing, because textbook publishers are the great cowards of the industry, there has, unfortunately, been some dilution of evolutionary content in many books. However, I think scientists have mobilized. They have been effective in courts, and particularly at the level of local battles and local school boards. Scientists, after all, are parents, too. Not that creationism is going away—it won't. It's a powerful political and social movement in America, but it is not a scientific movement.

LEAKEY: I would simply like to appeal to people hearing this discussion, not only here but elsewhere, to use that heritage of the large brain, intelligence, and recognize that this movement of scientific creationism is an absolute insult, both to religion and to science, and should be treated as such, with contempt.

STONE: I would only make this brief comment. I hope that you are right, my good friend, that the so-called creationists are self-defeating. If you would come out and live in southern

California, you might not enjoy that euphoria. I think we need to know that our future in the next half-century as Americans, as human beings, as intelligent creatures, is going to be determined by our ardor, our strength, and our determination to live intelligent, civilized lives for the rest of our time.

CHAIRMAN: I have a general question upon which several of you may want to comment. The proposition here is that man may have evolved too far, that our presumed intelligence may be our ultimate downfall as a species. Perhaps cultural Lamarckism and its transfer of information to future generations is in some ways to our detriment. What is our future in this nuclear age?

MEDAWAR: I do not understand the tendency, even the willingness to depreciate, even to deprecate, intelligence. Intelligence is our great strength. It is our only hope of the future. As my wife and I put it in the little book we wrote together, "Human beings are the only organisms that can find their way about the world by a light which illumines more than the patch of ground that we stand on." We have the possibility of anticipating what may happen in the future and of knowing what happened in the past. Upon this rests our hope of progress. Now why attempt to depreciate the importance of intelligence? It is our great source of strength, and to depreciate it is mere folly. It shows lack of intelligence or a lack of appreciation of intelligence.

PELIKAN: I find it, Sir Peter, particularly so, and therefore especially offensive when it is done in the name of faith in God, since it is the common consent of Jewish and Christian traditions that intelligence is itself the image of God.

MEDAWAR: Well spoken.

LEAKEY: It's a very difficult question to answer because there are so many imponderables. But let me just make a few remarks that would perhaps strengthen something I alluded to, but didn't go into. First of all, I don't think one can say that we've evolved too far. Nobody has said that. We have evolved very well to where we are. We, as a species, are quite successful at what we're doing at the moment. And I think you've got to think in terms of the species beyond the confines of either this state or this continent—to think in terms of the world. *Homo sapiens* has evolved satisfactorily in that sense. *Homo sapiens,* in relatively recent times, has evolved the capacity to develop not only nuclear arms, but other by-products of technology that are potentially extremely dangerous not only to our species, but to all other forms of life on this planet. Linked to that, we have developed the capacity to talk about it—hence, the question and the answer. We are aware of these dangers. We are aware of the potentials of misusing our technology. I think what is needed is essentially what this conference is doing—an understanding. We have the technological wherewithal; we have the knowledge to avoid the destruction of our species. We know how it can be achieved, and it's simply a question of using that knowledge, which is essentially political will. Political will will come through understanding, and understanding will come from knowing oneself. I think it would be a mistake to think we have evolved too far. We haven't evolved too far. We've evolved far enough to know the problem. And it's knowing the problem that will solve the problem.